CASTLES IN CUMBRIA

Carlisle Castle, the inner gatehouse

CASTLES
IN CUMBRIA

BY

JEAN M. COPE

CICERONE PRESS
2 POLICE SQUARE, MILNTHORPE, CUMBRIA

ISBN 1-85284-075-7

Contents

KEY TO MAPS

⟋⟋ Metalled Roads	■ Building
– – – – Tracks	☐ Ruin
· – – – Paths	
•—— Railways	◯ Sea or Lake
～～ Rivers	

Introduction

CUMBRIA IS A region where fighting continued regularly for much longer than it did in the rest of the country. Consequently it is possible to see the fortifications that were used for attack and defence over a long period of time. We have examples of Iron Age forts, Roman forts, Norman castles and pele towers, the fortresses of the lesser nobility, all within a reasonably limited area. In Cumbria, it is possible to trace the developments in warfare which took place by looking at the fortifications of different ages. Some of them are in a good state of repair, some are in ruins and it is only possible to detect the sites of some others. Yet most are in remarkable situations and even visiting ruins can be a fascinating experience.

A fortification can have two main purposes. It can be defensive; it can provide a place to which one can retreat and remain in safety. Alternatively, it can be offensive; it can be a base where troops can be lodged, from which they can emerge to attack or control the surrounding country. Some satisfy both functions. The siting of fortifications depends partly on which purpose is more important, but it depends also on the nature of warfare at the time.

It seems that the purpose of Iron Age forts was primarily defensive. They were mostly built on hills which were easy to defend and commanded a good visibility. The tribes of a particular area could have withdrawn into the fort with their stock in times of danger. These were fortifications built by a group of people for their own defence. Roman forts and Norman castles often occupy very similar sites; indeed, it is sometimes the same site. The Romans and the Normans were concerned with policing the region. Their fortresses were built at strategic points on important routes which enabled them to exert control over the neighbouring countryside. Roman forts and Norman castles were part of a national pattern, planned by a central government. Pele towers were different again. They were the fortified homes of individuals and were built at random as members of the lesser nobility decided they needed some protection. The towers can be found almost anywhere but there tends to be a concentration on the routes favoured by their attackers. This is self-defence, not military planning on a national scale.

The Romans fought in the open so the defences of their forts were not elaborate, a good site and wide gates were the main essentials so that the troops could move out of the fort quickly. Sometimes there is evidence of change in the buildings. Sites which had been fortified were deserted at a later stage, even though the area was still occupied by the Romans. Excavation has shown that such forts were built during the period when the Romans first conquered the north of the country, they were deserted at a later date and then occupied again. This seems to have coincided with the Roman attempt to conquer Scotland which was eventually abandoned. Hadrian's Wall became the effective frontier of the Empire and the forts in Cumbria became important again. Similarly, it is thought that the Cumbrian coast forts were built as a response to attacks from Ireland. In such cases a political decision resulted in a change in military strategy.

The Normans made similar decisions. Many mottes can be seen which were built as the Normans established their control of the country. After a while, permanent stone keeps were built at strategic points in the region whilst the remainder was abandoned. This was a political decision made by a king.

Kings soon realised that too many castles in the hands of disloyal nobles could be a threat to their own power, so a noble had to have permission to crenellate (fortify) his abode and only the king could give this permission. The king controlled the location and number of castles for royal security was of paramount importance.

Developments in military science also caused change. Many styles of building can be seen in most castles because different parts have been added or altered throughout the time in which they were used. There was a constant struggle between attackers and defenders to outwit each other. As castles had the dual roles of home and fortification, the desire for greater comfort resulted in constant modification. The final change took place when the use of artillery made the castle redundant as a weapon of war. Some remained in use as prisons or the barracks of a modern army and some were adapted to become stately homes. Those which could not be adapted for any other purpose became a useful source of raw materials for the local populace and gradually declined into the many ruins we can see today.

The need to defend this part of the country for so long was due to the long struggle between the Scots and the English for domination. Fighting in Iron Age times was probably between neighbouring tribes for there was no concept of nationality at this time. The Romans never established their authority over the tribes north of Hadrian's Wall. There were long periods of peace but there were also many incursions by the Picts and the Scots. The most intense and organised fighting was in the Middle Ages. From the Norman Conquest to the accession of James I in 1603, there were rarely long periods without strife. Once England and Scotland became recognisable countries, the kings of both of them wished to include the counties of the present north of England in their kingdoms. Sometimes one was successful, sometimes the other. Most kings of England maintained that the Scottish kings owed them allegiance but most Scottish kings tried to deny this. Each took advantage of any sign of weakness in the other and invaded at every possible opportunity.

In 1092, William II of England established the border north of Carlisle. However, in the Civil War between Stephen and Matilda, David I of Scotland was an ally of Matilda and he took advantage of the war to extend his kingdom and ruled Cumbria until his death. Henry II won back all the northern counties and forced David's successor, Malcolm IV, to renounce his claims. When there was a contested accession to the Scottish throne in the thirteenth century, Edward I, 'the Hammer of the Scots', asserted his suzerainty over Scotland. He made considerable inroads into its territory and even removed the Stone of Scone. However, Edward II had not his father's ability and soon lost the Battle of Bannockburn to Robert the Bruce. After this resounding victory, Robert ravaged the northern counties of England for many years.

The struggle continued in this manner through the centuries. Each country remained a threat to the other and caused much misery and hardship in the lands where the fighting took place. It is said that the town of Berwick-on-Tweed changed nationality thirteen times. Henry VIII's victory at Flodden finally gave the advantage to England but the ultimate cause of peace was the end of the line of Tudor monarchs. James VI of Scotland realised he could extend his kingdom peacefully by his rightful claim to the English throne and so fighting the English became unnecessary.

Unfortunately, the ambition of monarchs was only one cause of aggression in the Border Counties. Fighting had become a way of life which continued even when the kingdoms were not at war and it became almost impossible to control. It might be caused by long standing feuds between Border families or it might be straightforward cattle rustling. Lords and commoners alike were involved in the raiding. The members of each band might be occupied full-time with raiding or they might combine an occasional foray with some other occupation. They knew each other well and had a strong bond of loyalty although they were not necessarily of one nationality as cross-border membership was quite common. Above all, reivers had the same abilities; they had courage, strength and cunning, a remarkable knowledge of the countryside and the skill to ride great distances at night with ease. Autumn was the main season for their attacks when the harvest had been taken in and riding was easier. Conditions were ideal for their purposes, for the cattle were still in the fields. They carried out their plans quickly, rounded up their chosen target and made for home without delay, dealing with any opposition ruthlessly.

The chronicler Froissart described their activities with some admiration: 'When they enter England, within a day and night they will drive their whole host twenty-four mile. They take with them no purveyance of bread or wine for their usage and soberness is such that they will pass in the journey a great long time with flesh half sodden, without bread, and drink the river water without wine'. No doubt the English reivers were similarly admirable.

Efforts were made by the English and the Scots to keep some control of their unruly subjects. The Borders were divided into three regions for administrative purposes and both Scots and English had Eastern, Middle and Western Marches, which were under the control of a Warden and assistants. The English Marches were centred at Berwick-on-Tweed, Harbottle and Carlisle.

The Wardens were usually members of the leading families of each country. Wardens had many duties, but their prime task was to maintain law and order in their territory. They had to hold all necessary courts and sessions and administer any punishments which were given and were in charge of all strategic castles. They had to provide a system of watches and beacons so that they were in a position to deal with any trouble and had to suggest possible reforms to the system, so a thorough knowledge of their March was absolutely essential.

The two nations did attempt to co-operate to lessen the disorder in the region. Once a month there was a Day of Truce when the two sides met and tried to sort out problems. The two Wardens agreed a suitable day, a truce was declared from sunrise to sunset and they met, at an agreed venue. They each brought a set number of supporters, usually 1,000, and each was required to come in peace with only a sword or knife as a weapon. The purpose of the day was to settle all current grievances and the Wardens were supposed to part amicably. They usually did so, although there were violent exceptions when some hot-blooded follower managed to create a disturbance which led to a general skirmish.

The issues that were considered were often concerned with the disputed ownership of cattle or other accusations of robbery. They might be settled by combat but there were other odd customs, such as the driving of cattle into the Rivers Tweed or Esk to establish ownership. It was not easy for a Warden to establish the truth of a case and see that justice was done, because witnesses were hard to find as the fear of revenge was a powerful deterrent. Most men preferred to protest ignorance even if they had suffered some loss as they knew too well the probable consequence of assisting the law.Better to be impoverished but alive! The victim of a raid did have several options if he wished to take some action. He could complain to the Warden, although this was the action of a weak man, or he could merely wait and plan a raid in reprisal. Border folk knew each other well and this was commonly done. The third option was known as the 'hot trod' and was an accepted legal process.

The hot trod allowed the man to pursue the thieves and recover his property by whatever means were necessary. There were strict rules that had to be followed to make it plain this was not a mere raid of reprisal but was a legal response. The pursuit had to take place within six days of the attack and if the victim had to cross the border in his pursuit, he was supposed to carry a burning turf on a lance so that everyone he met would be aware of his purpose. A trod was not an easy option because the raiders' intimate knowledge of the countryside enabled them to hide in the numerous gullies and ravines of this wild region. However, the thieves were encumbered by a herd of cattle which would not move rapidly and the victim also knew the locality well. It was regarded as quite understandable if a hot trod ended in the death of one or more of the attackers. Unfortunately it was sometimes the victim who suffered, not his enemies.

If the Wardens did not succeed in keeping the peace in their march by the usual means, there was a general call to arms. All able-bodied men and boys had to respond unless they had some good reason. There were look-outs at strategic points, such as fords where the reivers might cross a river or along the 'thievs' rodes' they would be likely to use. Leading members of the community were responsible for maintaining an efficient system and, when they had advance warning of an attack pending, they were supposed to inform the Warden. The alarm was spread by the beacons which were sited on suitable hills and on all available towers. Castles and pele towers were obliged to display a warning fire and so news of the attack was relayed to a wide area quickly.

There was one area of land which became known as the Debatable Land because neither country would concede its ownership to the other. It was only a small area, about twelve miles by four miles stretching south from Langholm to the Solway Moss but it became the domain of the worst elements in the Borders. The families who lived there were almost beyond the law. Both countries would mount expeditions to devastate the land from time to time. The offending reivers and their families would go into hiding, only to return to their homes and their thieving ways once the arm of the law had departed. Eventually, in the middle of the sixteenth century Scotland and England decided a solution to this imponderable problem had to be found. In 1552, the French ambassador held a meeting of all concerned and a decision was made. The Debatable Land was divided between the two countries and a ditch and a bank were built from east to west to mark the boundary. The Scots Dyke still marks the line today.

There must have been great relief when King James insisted that the Borders were pacified and that Border folk must live in peace like the rest of the country. No doubt it would now at last be possible for life to develop normally in the north of England and the south of Scotland. The varied means of defence were no longer necessary, but many can still be seen and are a fascinating commentary on a long struggle between very determined people.

One: Iron Age Forts

IRON AGE FORTS are mainly associated with the Celts who spread westward from their eastern European homelands around 1200-700 B.C. and probably first came to this country in the early seventh century B.C. The Celts were not a literate people, so the only comments we have on their society come from classical writers. Julius Caesar and others wrote about their ferocity in battle and their generally barbaric culture: "They live on milk and meat and wear skins'; 'they wear their hair long and shave the whole of their bodies except the head and the upper lip'; 'they dye their bodies with woad which produces a blue colour'; 'their relationships are polygamous and they have no cities only a few towns'. These observations coloured the views of Celts until the first archaeological excavations in the nineteenth century produced artefacts of such exquisite design and skilled craftmanship that a different view of Celtic society has emerged. They were people who delighted in beauty.

The study of hillforts has provided further evidence of their skills. The building of the largest and most complicated defences which have been identified could only be achieved by a people capable of controlled organisation and thought, fierce and fond of fighting though they may have been.

It has been estimated that more than 3,000 Iron Age forts have been identified in Britain. Sites have been found all over the country, although most are to be found in the south of England and in parts of Wales and Scotland. Few sites have been extensively excavated, but it seems that they were built and used during the thousand years of the first millennium B.C. The idea of building a fence or wall round your home as a defence against wild animals or enemies is a fairly basic one, and there are many examples from the Bronze Age. Settlements have been found which have been surrounded by a raised bank which probably supported a wooden palisade. The Iron Age fort is an obvious extension of this idea.

The forts vary in some of their details but most were built on a hilltop or promontory. There is a great range of size; the smallest occupy half an acre or less, whilst the largest may cover more than 60 or 70 acres. Evidence of human habitation has been found in only some of them. The small enclosures may well have been the homes of just one family and its stock, whilst the larger ones may be considered as villages or towns. Although it is assumed that most were occupied continually, some might have been used seasonally, some might have been intended primarily for stock, while others might have been used only in an emergency.

All of the forts have defences of some sort. The 'univallate', defence consists of a bank of earth which probably supported a palisade rather like the Bronze Age defences or a similarly simple stone wall, whilst the most advanced forts, the 'multivallate', have a series of banks and ditches which cover a considerable area. In all forts the entrance was clearly an important feature. In some cases, it is merely a definite opening in the wall or bank which could have been blocked in some way, perhaps with lengths of timber or even with thorn bushes. In the most advanced forts, the entrance has become an example of advanced military engineering with staggered tunnels and guard-houses. In either case, it is clear that the intention of the builders was to maintain strict control over entry to the fort.

The design of each fort must have depended on a variety of conditions. The choice of site was the first decision that had to be made. Of course, we cannot tell what freedom of choice these people had, but many forts

Hardknott Roman Fort
Hadrian's Wall, the granaries, Birdoswald

do seem to be built in the most obviously strategic situation, so we may assume that people had considerable freedom to choose the area in which they lived. The type of raw material available to the builders was obviously very important. The sort of defence constructed had to vary according to what was available. Where there is an ample supply of stone, as there is in Cumbria, there is little incentive to develop the complicated structures which can be found in the south of England. The size of fort must have depended on how many people there were to participate in the building process. The large forts suggest that many people did live in the neighbourhood.

Once these decisions had been made, a preliminary plan would have been marked out on the ground by stakes or by digging a shallow ditch. Then the main ditch would have been dug and the main rampart built. Five different designs have been identified - the contour fort, the promontory fort, the plateau fort, valley forts and hillslope forts. The last three do not have the obvious defensive advantages of the first two, but are still included in the description 'hillfort'. The contour fort, the classic fort of the Iron Age, is constructed by the defences following a contour round a hilltop. This is why some of them seem to be a rather strange shape. All the land within a particular contour become part of the fort. The hill did not have to be especially high - quite low hills were utilised in places - but all such sites provided a very strong defensive situation. The hillslope fort must have been one of the least efficient, as it could be attacked from above. It is possible that this type was used primarily for stock enclosures.

The earliest defences consisted of timber palisades on top of an earthen bank which had a ditch in front of it. However, timber can quickly succumb to fire and there were many experiments with different, more complex

Brougham Castle Photo: Walt Unsworth

designs to overcome this problem. In some forts, a double row of timber was built onto the bank, the uprights were strengthened with timber crossbars and the spaces in between were filled with rubble. Sometimes it seems that the exterior was covered with turf or even with stone to protect the wood that was still exposed. Sometimes there was a sloping or stepped rampart behind the timber to give it extra strength and to provide easy access to the top of the rampart for the defenders. Yet other experiments were made with steep slopes extending continuously from the bottom of the ditch to the top of the rampart and in some cases, sharp upturned stones have been found at the bottom of slopes, providing a sort of mantrap! There is almost no end to the ingenuity of these people in trying to improve the safety of their forts.

The most vulnerable part of the system of defence was the gateway. There was no alternative material to wood and wood can always be burnt by hurling flaming torches at it. A simple entrance was an easy prey to fire or battering, but once again modern investigations have exposed a variety of ingenious solutions. Many elaborate designs have been found. In some cases, where there were multiple ramparts, the way through was staggered to prevent a rush attack. In others, the openings were aligned, but a long passage was the only means of entrance: anyone wishing to enter had to endure considerable surveillance before he reached the interior. A further development was the building of barbicans or a forward projection of the ramparts by the entrance, once again improving the control of the defenders.

While the defences were very important for the existence of the fort, the living conditions inside were just as important for the people who had to live in them. Unfortunately, in many cases, it is impossible to discover what these conditions were, as there are no traces of them. This may mean that the fort was not actually lived in. Of course, it may mean that the material of the people's homes has rotted, leaving no trace. Tents made of animal skins or temporary wooden shacks with no foundations could completely disappear in time.

In the forts where evidence has been found, circles can be discerned on the ground. This probably means that the people lived in round huts, the circles marking the foundations. Typical huts were six to eight metres in diameter, although some as large as 15 metres have been discovered. Rings of posts are often discovered which would have supported the lining of the hut and the thatched roof. There would have been a central living space, with a hearth in the middle. The outer space might have had compartments made by hanging skins or boards from the roof. In some Scottish huts, stone divisions have been discovered inside and these suggest a possible pattern. The hut was often surrounded by a ditch for drainage and the door might have been a simple opening with a hanging curtain. Sometimes there seems to have been a more complex structure, with a passage for added protection.

If people lived in a fort continuously, they would have needed other buildings in addition to their homes. Where hillforts have been excavated, sometimes other patterns of post-holes have been found. It is thought that some of these could have been granaries, drying-racks or even hay-stacks. The preservation of food would have been important at all times, but especially in times of danger. In some cases, the holes make a pattern which suggests the existence of a large hall and so we might assume that this was the residence of an important chief - perhaps the fort was the headquarters of his people. In addition, pits are often found and again these might have been used for a variety of purposes. They could have been used for the storage of grain, water, anything else that had to be preserved or rubbish. Modern experiments have proved that this is an efficient method of storage. Sometimes human or animal remains in a pit suggest it was used for sacrifices. It is possible that some of the hillforts also had a religious purpose.

While the defences of the forts were obviously important. It is not clear whether they had to withstand sieges. In some cases it has been found that the gateway was burnt down and there have been some examples of mass graves, which would suggest massacres. However, these are unusual and evidence of great destruction is rare. Normally the Celts fought in the open. The classical writers refer to their expertise in fighting with chariots. They describe the noise of 'bellowing horns and screaming fighters' in which the Celts delighted and which presaged an attack on a rival force. The simplest method of attacking a hillfort was to drive the defenders off the ramparts by a shower of missiles. The attackers could then advance under their shields, undermine the ramparts and set fire to the gates. Timber revetments (retaining walls) could be fired and dry-stone walling might collapse. Incendiary darts and red-hot sling-stones could be hurled at the defenders. Of course, the defenders would also hurl their weapons and if the attack did not succeed quickly, it is probable that it was soon called off. Perhaps, then, the defenders would pour out of the fort to pursue their enemies as the slow pressure of a siege seems alien to the Celts. Archaeological evidence appears to confirm Caesar's account of Celtic warfare.

We cannot know exactly how people lived in hillforts, but clearly the defences of the hillforts were important to their safety, even if the actual fighting took place outside the fort. For a very long time, these forts were a normal part of life in most of Britain. It is apparent that this way of life came to an end when the Romans took control of the country in the first century A.D. In some cases, gaps in the defensive ramparts of the forts have been found. This suggests that someone intended the fortifications should not be used again. It is possible that this was a decision of a Roman commander, or perhaps, as the Romans built their towns and army camps the British themselves decided that the Roman way of life was more attractive. Whatever the reason, the Iron Age hillfort ceased to be a notable feature of life in Britain soon after the establishment of Roman rule. There may have been some reoccupation after the Romans left in the fifth century, but the evidence for this is fairly obscure. We do not know exactly how many forts were in use at this time nor for what reason they were occupied.

There are not many hillforts in the north-west and those that have been discovered, are mostly small and univallate - that is, their defences consist of a single wall or bank. One fort, Carrock Fell, is an exception because, although univallate, it covers five acres and is a noticeable feature in the landscape of the northern mountains in Cumbria. Some of the others are more difficult to identify. Few Iron Age artefacts have been discovered in the region, so it is difficult to know how extensive the population was at this time. A remarkable sword and its sheath, the Embleton sword, were discovered in the nineteenth century, near Wythop Mill, but this is an exception. There are many other signs of prehistoric people, such as henges, (prehistoric circles of massive stone or wood uprights), stone circles and Bronze Age settlements, but not many artefacts of the Iron Age. It is probable that these people were pastoral farmers and the population may have been very scattered, but we do not have a clear picture yet.

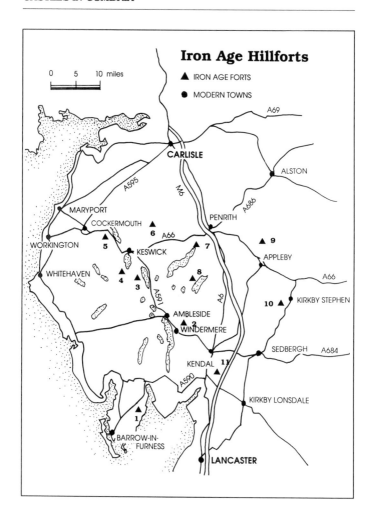

Iron Age Hillforts

▲ IRON AGE FORTS

● MODERN TOWNS

Gazeteer - The Iron Age

1. SKELMORE HEADS, GREAT URSWICK 97 274 752
The defences are univallate and enclose a trapezoidal area on the top of the hill. On three sides they consist of the natural rock escarpment but on the north there is a bank and ditch. These are now worn down and irregular but when they were investigated, it was found that the ditch was eight to nine feet wide and three feet deep. The bank was made of rubble and was separated from the ditch by a berm (a level area) four to five feet wide. The bank may have been strengthened in front (revetted) by upright timbers. There is a single entrance at the north west.

Directions Take the A590 from Ulverston to Barrow. One and a half miles from Ulverston take the left turn to Great Urswick. Turn left in the middle of the village, then second left along a lane up the hill to the fort, about half a mile.

IRON AGE FORTS

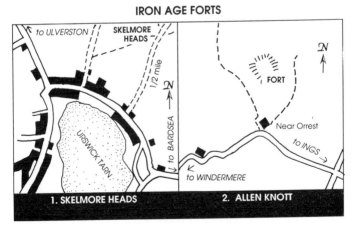

1. SKELMORE HEADS   2. ALLEN KNOTT

2. ALLEN KNOTT, WINDERMERE 90 420 005

Much of the site has been destroyed by quarrying and only the north west stretch of the rampart can be seen, it is about seven feet high in places. The fort was roughly rectangular in shape.

Directions Take the A591 from Windermere to Ambleside. After half a mile turn right at the roundabout and take the A592 to Penrith. After another half a mile take the second turning on the right to Ings. After about one mile, on the left is a path beside Near Orrest farm which passes near the fort.

3. CASTLE CRAG, THIRLMERE 90 298 190

On the far side of Raven Crag, it has a good natural position but is difficult to reach and the remains are slight.

Directions Take the A591 from Keswick to Ambleside. Three and a half miles from Keswick turn right along the lake road. After half a mile there is a path in the woodland on the right going sharply up the hill over the ridge to the

IRON AGE FORTS

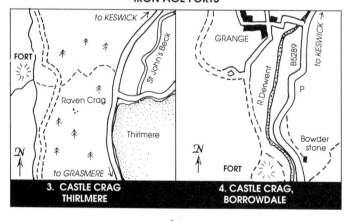

3. CASTLE CRAG
THIRLMERE

4. CASTLE CRAG,
BORROWDALE

fort. The summit of Raven Crag is through the woods to the left. A series of wooden arrows on posts mark the path to the fort.

4.   CASTLE CRAG, BORROWDALE 90 250 160
Across the road from the Bowder Stone, this is another good defensive situation on the top of a small hill but the remains have been damaged by quarrying. The top is about 60 yards in diameter and access to it is narrow with only room for one man to pass. A girdle of rubble ramparts is visible.

Directions Take the B5289 from Keswick to Borrowdale. At the end of Derwentwater, turn right to Grange. From Grange a path can be followed to the top of the hill. There is also a car park by the Bowder Stone but there is some difficulty in crossing the River Derwent from here.

5.   CASTLE HOW, BASSENTHWAITE 90 202 308
This fort is adjacent to the lake on a steep crag. It is

IRON AGE FORTS

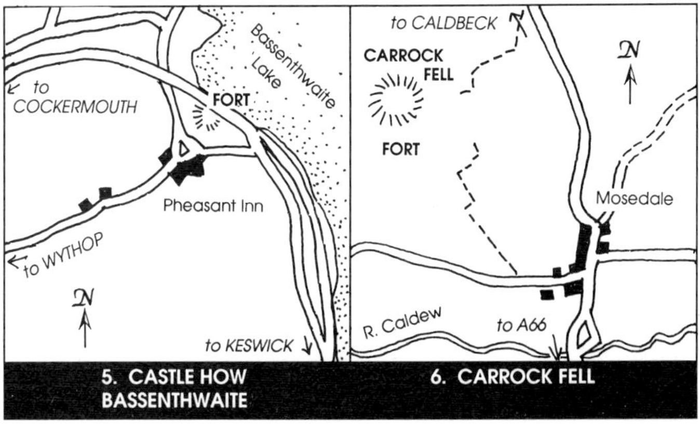

5. CASTLE HOW
BASSENTHWAITE

6. CARROCK FELL

25

Carrock Fell Iron Age Fort

unusual for Cumbria as it is multivallate. There are four lines of ramparts on the west and two on the east where the steepness of the slope gives extra protection.

Directions Take the A66 from Keswick to Cockermouth. At the end of the lake, turn left to Wythop Mill. The fort is on the hill on the right between the lane and the main road.

6.   CARROCK FELL, MUNGRISDALE 90 342 337
This is by far the largest and most impressive hillfort in Cumbria and can be seen from all parts of Inglewood Forest. It is a contour fort and univallate. The defensive rampart surrounds an irregular double summit 800ft by 370ft and has an area of five acres. The rampart is over eight foot thick and is intact in places. There are two gateways. The south gate leads to a spring whilst the west gateway is built of massive blocks of stone and was possibly the main entrance. There are other gaps in the

26

rampart which seem to have been made deliberately, as the stones which have been moved can be seen further down the hill. The fort has not been excavated. There is an oval cairn on the east summit, but there are no signs of huts. A settlement in the valley below has been excavated and three different types of hut and human remains were discovered.

Directions Take the A66 from Penrith to Keswick. About nine miles from Penrith, turn right to Mungrisdale and Caldbeck. After three miles the village of Mosedale is reached and there are three paths which ascend the hill. For the steepest but most direct path, turn left in Mosedale along the road to Swineside and take a path up the hill to the right. At the end of the buildings, a slightly easier beginning can be made from the Caldbeck road. For a slightly less steep but longer path, turn left in Mosedale towards Swineside and take a diagonal, green path on the right after about a mile.

7. DUNMALLET FORT, POOLEY BRIDGE 90 468 247

This is a small, oval fort covering about one acre but it is difficult to distinguish because of the trees which cover it. However, there are paths which go right to the top from which there is a fine view of Ullswater. It is a univallate fort and the gap on the south west is probably the original gateway.

Directions Take the A66 from Penrith to Keswick. After one mile, turn left on the A592 to Windermere. After three and a half miles, turn left on the B5320 to Pooley Bridge. There is a parking place on the left, within a few hundred yards, before you cross the river to the village. The path to the fort leads from it.

8. CASTLE CRAG, HAWESWATER 90 469 128

Castle Crag is well sited below Birks Crag and now overlooks Haweswater, although this was a dry valley. The crags give it a natural defence, but there are also rock-cut ditches.

Directions Take the A6 from Penrith. After half a mile, turn right on the B5320 to Pooley Bridge. After one mile and crossing the railway bridge, fork left in Yanwath on the road to Askham, Helton and Bampton. Fork right in Bampton on the Haweswater road and drive to the end of the lake. From the car park, take the lakeside path to the far side of the lake and follow it round past The Rigg and across Riggindale Beck. Birk Crag and the fort are on the next slope on your left and can be reached by a scramble up from the lakeside path.

IRON AGE FORTS

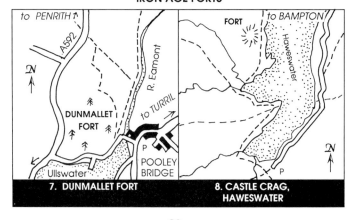

7. DUNMALLET FORT

8. CASTLE CRAG, HAWESWATER

9.   DUFTON HILLFORT 91 702 230

The site is on Castle Hill and is roughly circular in shape. It covers about one acre. The defences consist of a bank and an external ditch. There are entrance gaps to the north-east and north-west. There are a number of hut circles and a square enclosure to the south-west.

Directions Take the B6542 from the middle of Appleby. On the edge of the town, turn right under the railway bridge and the A66, on the minor road to Brampton and Dufton. After about two miles, a footpath on the right leads up the hill, through a wood. The settlement is on the top of the hill.

10. CROGLAM CASTLE, KIRKBY STEPHEN 91 768 077

This is an oval enclosure of about one and a half acres. The defences consist of a ditch and an external bank. There is an entrance gap at the north-east. No hut foundations or other features are visible.

IRON AGE FORTS

| 9. DUFTON | 10. CROGLAM CASTLE |

Directions Take the A685 to Tebay from the centre of Kirkby Stephen. After passing the left fork to Nateby B6259, take the next small turning on the right. This leads to a road parallel to the A685. Turn left along this road and continue about half a mile. A path on the left leads to the fort.

11. CASTLESTEADS FORT, NATLAND 97 530 887

This is a small oval fort on Helm Hill. There is a ditch and two banks which are most obvious on the north and the south. There is a steep drop on the east which provides a natural defence.

Directions From Kendal take the A65 to Endmoor for about one and a half miles. Soon after crossing the railway, there is a parking place on the left. From here, paths lead up the hill. Keep to the right-hand path at first. This is a very steep climb, but it leads straight to the fort.

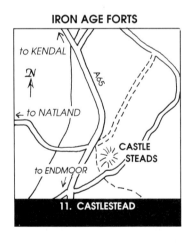

IRON AGE FORTS

11. CASTLESTEAD

Two: Roman Forts

JULIUS CÆSAR LANDED twice in Britain, in 55 and 56 B.C. but the lasting invasion and occupation of the country occurred in 43 A.D. under the Emperor Claudius. There was opposition from the various British tribes he encountered in the south of the country, but the lowland zone was overrun within four years. There was a further thrust northwards from 61-84 A.D. when Agricola pushed far into Scotland with a victory at Mons Graupius near the north-east coast. Scotland was never really controlled, although efforts were made to contain the Picts and the Scots from time to time. Hadrian's Wall was built in 128 A.D. on the instructions of the Emperor, probably after he visited Britain in 121 A.D. It was built across the lands of the Brigantes but became the permanent limit of Roman power in Britain.

Within the area they controlled, the Romans organised life as they had done elsewhere in the Empire. The land and people were divided into a number of 'civitates' which sometimes corresponded with the natural area of one of the British tribes. The leading members of the tribe became the council for the civitas and had to deal with all matters of local government. Of course, the whole country was under the rule of a Roman governor and the Roman Army kept the peace, but the Britons were absorbed into the system of government of the country and many of them became increasingly Romanised in their way of life. Roads were built as soon as an area was pacified and forts and signalling towers were constructed so that the Roman army could control any opposition which might arise.

Towns were built in the Roman style with shops and public buildings and there was soon a thriving economic life. Various goods were manufactured in this country, many were imported from the Continent and there was a widespread use of coinage. In some parts of the country splendid villas were built for the aristocracy who soon adapted to a Roman lifestyle. Roman civilisation was accepted for nearly four hundred years but eventually the threat of the barbarians resulted in the withdrawal of the Roman forces. In 410 A.D. the Emperor Honorius told the British to look after their own defences and in 450 A.D. the plea to the Emperor Aetius for help met with no response.

Throughout the period of Roman rule, the north-west was primarily a military region with a complex of roads and defences covering the whole of it. The main road in any region connected the principal forts - in north-west England these were Chester and York - and they determined the main lines of communication. The road system gave the army access to the whole region and connected the forts to the south and to Scotland during the period when the Romans occupied part of it. The main road in north-west England linked Chester to Carlisle and passed through Ribchester, Burrow-in-Lonsdale, Tebay and Brougham. This was the military road traversing the western slopes of the Pennines. At a later date, a second north-south road was built from Chester going through Warrington, Wigan, Walton-le-Dale, The Fylde, Garstang and Lancaster. The main road was linked to Ermine Street and thence to York by Stanegate (Carlisle to Corbridge) and to Catterick through Brough and the Stainmore Gate. A further route led from Brougham to Ambleside and thence over Hardknott to Ravenglass and connected the system to the coast. Finally, a coastal road connected Hadrian's Wall with the coastal forts from Bowness-on-Solway, as far south as Moresby.

The Roman fort was a key factor in the control of any country and some sort of fortification was built at regular intervals along the main roads. The main forts were built at strategic points such as a river confluence or crossing,

Pendragon Castle

Egremont Castle

or perhaps a well-placed headland. There were many smaller ones also, but not all that have been identified were in use throughout the Romans' occupation. Changing conditions resulted in different deployments of troops and sometimes a particular threat resulted in a change of defence. It is thought that the forts down the Cumbrian coast were built to deal with coastal raids by the Scots. The final withdrawal of the Romans from Scotland altered permanently the strategic thinking for the whole area.

When the army was on the move, marching camps were established when it was necessary to stop, but these did not always become permanent fortifications. The marching camp could be built quickly as the process was simple: a ditch was dug round a rectangular area, an earthen rampart was thrown up with a wooden palisade erected on top of it and then the soldiers pitched leather tents in the enclosed space. If the camp was not required for a permanent fort, it could easily be abandoned. When permanent sites were selected, the forts were built in a similar manner, but wooden and stone buildings replaced the leather tents. Many were rectangular, but the shape did vary slightly according to the site. Obviously the strategic position was the key factor, as the shape of the land available was not necessarily ideal. The main features were similar to those of the marching camps; the main shape was more or less rectangular with a tower at each rounded corner. Each side had a turreted gateway to allow easy and rapid movement of the troops and the surrounding wall was about 14-15ft high and often supported by a turf mound with a rampart. There was a ditch outside the wall and a roadway inside it, to give access to the rampart.

The Roman Army included all the specialists needed for the building of roads and military installations. Each

Kendal Castle Photo: Walt Unsworth

legion had its own surveyors, architects, engineers, masons and carpenters. Once an area had been conquered, the strategic position of a fort was identified. The main requirement was a site which gave a good view of the surrounding neighbourhood, but also allowed the army easy access. A strongly defensive situation was not necessary. The Roman army was on the offensive, its main task was to police the region so it needed primarily to be able to get out of the fort easily. A water supply was essential and many forts are to be found on low hills near a stream or river.

When such a site had been located, the construction could start. The land might have to be cleared of trees - it is not known how much of Britain had already been deforested by the Celts - and then the surveyors would have marked out the plans on the ground. When they were satisfied that the site was suitable, the ditch was dug, the rampart built and finally the buildings were constructed. Skilled craftsmen were necessary for this work and specialist tools similar to those still used, such as compasses, files, saws and planes, have been discovered at some forts. The ordinary labouring was done by the soldiers and construction tools such as shovels and axes were part of their normal equipment. Local materials were used wherever possible and certainly in Cumbria there must have been a plentiful supply of wood and stone. If there was no suitable roofing material, a tilery was soon established to provide the necessary tiles.

The interiors of the forts were also built to a standard pattern. Four streets led from the four gates and divided the fort into sections. All the important buildings were contained in the middle section. This was called the 'Principia' and was the spiritual and administrative centre of the fort. It consisted of ranges of buildings built round a courtyard where special parades or ceremonies were held. The central room at the rear was the focal point of the headquarters - it was called the 'aedes ' and was a shrine where a statue of the emperor stood. The unit's standard was kept here, and there was sometimes an altar and occasionally an underground strongroom as the aedes was guarded by a sentry at all times. The basilica was a large hall where the whole legion could assemble and the commander could issue general orders and deal with defaulters.

Other buildings were necessary for the administration of army affairs, but the next largest building was the 'Praetorium', the commander's residence. It was elaborately planned, with underfloor heating and a small bath-house and it might also have served as an officers' mess. In some forts, a hospital and the granaries, 'the horrea', were in the central complex. It was important to keep the corn safe and dry, and especial care was taken in siting and building the horrea. At the Ambleside fort, strong buttresses can be seen as part of the granary building which presumably supported a heavy roof, whilst low walls supported a hung floor for good ventilation.

The other two parts of the fort were the 'praetentura' or front portion and the 'retentura' or rear portion. These areas contained the barrack-blocks and the stabling. The barrack-blocks were grouped in pairs and each accommodated centuries of 80 men each. Each small section of eight men occupied two rooms for their stores and sleeping quarters and these were connected by an outside veranda. The centurion's quarters were at the end of each block and were slightly larger. Workshops, smithies, storehouses, cookhouses and ovens might also be built in the fort. Usually there was a small prison by the gate and sometimes an amphitheatre outside the wall. The latrines were usually by the ramparts in the lowest part of the fort and were flushed by water if possible, whilst the baths were outside the wall to decrease the risk of fire from the furnaces. The parade ground was also outside the walls and here there were parades on important occasions. Fitness was important for the troops so they were drilled regularly if they were not likely to be in combat for a while.

Hadrian's Wall was part of the general defensive structure of the North-West and its forts were built in a similar manner. At first, the wall itself was constructed of stone for two-thirds of its length from the eastern end and of turf and timber for the rest. The wall had a ditch to the north and milecastles every Roman mile, with two square turrets between each pair. Later forts were built on the Wall, the turf was replaced by stone and the vallum was built on the south side of it. This was a ditch with steep sides and berms north and south, bounded by continuous banks of earth. It provided a military zone 120ft wide overall and it has been estimated that 11,500 troops were required to guard it.

We have detailed knowledge of the organisation of the Roman army. There were three main branches: the Praetorian guard, the legions and the auxiliary legions. The Praetorian Guard was the imperial bodyguard and travelled everywhere with the Emperor. The legions were the elite of the army. They consisted solely of Roman citizens and were stationed usually at the frontier.

Legionary soldiers were highly trained and very tough. They were expected to be able to march 20 miles a day in about five hours, to set up camp at the end of it and be prepared for battle at all times. On the march they were fully laden with provisions for three days, tools for digging and building as well as their bronze helmets, leather shields, swords and spears. These men were the cream of the Roman army, the key fighters. There were also auxiliaries, native fighters who were led originally by their own chieftains. Their duties might consist of operations not vital enough for the legions or they might screen the legions in battle, in the front or on the flanks. Each legion was divided into various units; the smallest was the 'contubernium', the tent party of eight men - ten contubernii made a century, six centuries made a cohort and ten cohorts made a legion, about 5,300 fighting men and 700 support men in all.

Although their main task was to police the region, the presence of so many troops had other far-reaching effects on the British community. Soon after forts were completed, a civilian settlement, the 'vicus', developed outside many of them. These existed primarily to provide services for the troops, and they consisted of a variety of buildings. Some of the buildings were houses, possibly homes for the families of the troops, then there were shops, where the soldiers could buy things they required and other buildings where they would find entertainment in periods of peace, such as taverns, gambling dens and brothels. There was often a bathhouse and a temple and sometimes a 'mansio', the posting-house where official visitors could stay.

There would have been plenty of work for particular craftsmen - the blacksmith would have had an important role in a military community with weapons, helmets and body armour to be made and repaired. There was probably a steady demand for leather goods, for shoes, for shields, for horse trappings. In many ways, the vicus was like a medieval village, except that its existence depended entirely on the existence of the fort. The fort probably provided protection for the vicus and prosperity for its inhabitants, but the vicus must have made life much more agreeable for the inhabitants of the fort.

The presence of such large numbers of troops also had a considerable effect on the countryside. It is probable that the majority of the natives remained farmers as they had always been, but their farming practices must have changed as a ready market for surplus products appeared. It seems that most farms were mixed arable-pasture but they had to produce a certain amount of grain as a tax requirement. Any surplus grain or meat could be sold to the Romans, a major change in the lifestyle of the Britons. The farms were mostly single farmsteads, joined by tracks to the main roads. There must also have been extensive work in the forests, with the demand for wood for building and for the furnaces for the Romans' baths and heating systems.

It is thought that some of the farms which have been excavated in the region may have belonged to military veterans who settled here at the end of their military careers. When each soldier had completed his term of service, he was entitled to a grant of land in a colonia. He was given a diploma certifying his good service and a small cash grant which was usually sufficient to set him up in a farm. Many soldiers stayed near their old forts in the areas they had grown used to, and it is likely that many of the legionnaires who had manned the forts of north-west England, must have settled in this way and become part of the local community.

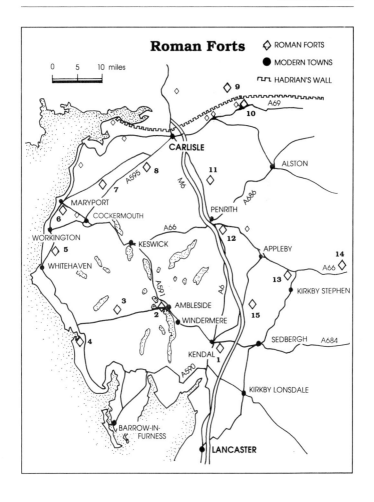

Roman Forts

◇ ROMAN FORTS
● MODERN TOWNS
ᒥᒲᒥ HADRIAN'S WALL

0   5   10 miles

Gazeteer - Roman Forts

In many cases, the sites of the Roman forts in the North West can only be seen on aerial photographs as patterns on the ground. The defences of some others are clearly visible but not very interesting, as they consist only of a slightly raised bank in the typical playing card shape. The known forts are marked on the map but the gazeteer describes in detail only those which are interesting to the layman. Museums in the region contain artefacts which have been recovered over many years from the sites of forts and from other sites and these give an added understanding of the way of life of the inhabitants of the forts and of the vici. These include altars dedicated to a variety of gods, inscriptions, tools and weapons, objects of everyday use such as pottery, jewellery, cooking utensils and many other things.

ROMAN FORTS

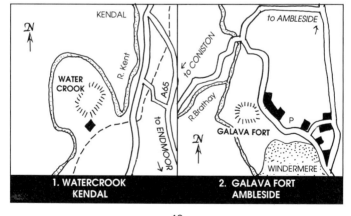

1. WATERCROOK, KENDAL 97 516 907

This fort consists of a raised platform of about three and a half acres, in a bend of the river south of the town. Few features can be identified. There are many artefacts in Kendal museum from excavations and from chance finds.

Directions Take the A65 south of the town towards Endmoor. After 200 yards, fork right to Natland. After half a mile, a path on the right leads to a farm and the site of the fort.

2. AMBLESIDE 90 373 035

Two forts have been identified south of the town on a promontory jutting into Windermere. The shape of one of them can be seen with the foundations of towers at the north-west and north-east corners, the Principia (the headquarters), the Praetorium (the commander's residence) and the horrea (the granaries). In the Principia it is possible to discern the basilica, a long covered hall, the tribunal, a raised dais for the commander, and the aedes, the chapel of standards which contains a small, sunken strongroom, approached by a flight of stairs. The horrea have massive external buttresses which would have supported a heavy roof, and a wooden floor would have rested on the grid-iron of low sill walls and there are ventilation holes between the buttresses on the base walls. Finds from the fort and the adjoining area can be seen in the Armitt Museum in Ambleside and in Tullie House Museum, Carlisle.

Directions At Waterhead south of the town, walk 200 yards along the lakeside road. On the left, there is a gate into the park which leads to the fort.

3. HARDKNOTT 89 225 015

Standing high on the mountainside overlooking Scafell, this has been described as one of the most spectacular forts in Europe. It is at an intermediate point on the road between Ambleside and Ravenglass and its purpose was to patrol and police this important route. It is a three acre site, the walls follow the contours and stand several feet high. The angle-towers can be seen clearly and it is thought that they contained store-rooms in the base and sentry rooms above. The foundations of the Principia, Praetorium and the horrea are all in place and there are traces of barrack blocks. The bath-house is outside the main entrance and the range of rooms is typical and well preserved. A path leads from the east gate to the parade ground, a large flattened area with a tribunal on the north edge - this is the best example surviving in Britain.

Directions From Ambleside, take the A593 to Coniston. After about four miles, take a minor road on the right, sign-posted Little Langdale. Drive over Wrynose and Hardknott Passes, about nine miles. The fort is on the right, about 200 yards over the top of the pass.

ROMAN FORTS

3. HARDKNOTT   4. WALLS CASTLE

Walls Castle, Ravenglass. The Roman bath-house

4. WALLS CASTLE, RAVENGLASS 96 087 958

The site of the fort was partly destroyed by the construction of the railway and most of what remains is covered by a plantation of trees. However, the bath house, which is known as Walls Castle, still stands to a height of twelve feet. Doorways into several rooms are obvious and there are some niches in the walls, but the exact purpose of each part is not precisely known.

Directions Take the A595 south from Whitehaven, about 16 miles. At a T-junction the main road turns left up the hill, the right turn leads to Ravenglass. Follow the Ravenglass road. On a bend before the railway bridge a small turning on the left leads to the fort.

5. MORESBY 89 963 210

The fort platform can be seen but it is partly covered by the churchyard.

Directions   Take the A595 north from Whitehaven to Parton, about two miles. At the end of the village, take a left turn. The fort is on the left after about 200 yards, the church is on the east side of the site.

6. MARYPORT   89 038 373

A five and a half acre site, the fort overlooks the sea on high ground to the north of the modern town. It was defended by a double ditch and a stone wall and the position of the four gates can be seen. There was a levelled parade ground with a tribunal to the south of the fort. Buildings from a vicus have been found and there are many artefacts in local museums.

Directions   From the museum in the centre of Maryport, take the road leading NNE for half a mile. A path on the left leads to the fort.

7. CAERMOTE   90 202 367

The outlines of two forts can be discerned, a three and a

ROMAN FORTS

5. MORESBY   6. MARYPORT

half acre site and a small fortlet in its north-west corner.

Directions From Keswick, take the A591 to Bothel. About two miles before Bothel, turn right towards Torpenhow. The fort is beside the road on the left, after half a mile.

8. OLD CARLISLE 85 260 465

The fort platform is clearly visible. The vicus is only apparent in aerial photographs, although there are records of its remains being seen in the 18th century. It was a large, important fort; many artefacts have been found and can be seen in Carlisle Museum.

Directions From Wigton take the B5304 south for one and a half miles. The fort is in a field on the left.

9. BEWCASTLE 86 566 747

This was one of the outposts of Hadrian's Wall and it was joined directly by road to Birdoswald Fort. It consists of an irregular, hexagonal six acre site. The external ditch can be seen and excavations uncovered the foundations of

ROMAN FORTS

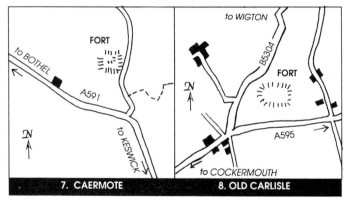

several buildings. The medieval castle was built in the north-east corner of the fort and the church and famous cross are also within the fort boundaries.

Directions From Brampton take the A69 east for half a mile. Turn left on a minor road to Lanercost for two miles. At the T-junction, turn right. After one mile the road forks left and leads to the hamlet of Bewcastle, about nine miles. At the road junction, a track on the right leads to the fort and the Norman castle.

10. BIRDOSWALD 86 615 663

This is the only fort on Hadrian's Wall in Cumbria where there are substantial remains to be seen. It is sited on the top of the escarpment above the Irthing valley and has extensive views over the valley. Hadrian's Wall originally abutted the two northern corners of the fort and can be seen winding away to the east.

The shape of the fort platform is clearly marked by the external wall and the four main gates and two minor gates

ROMAN FORTS

| 9. BEWCASTLE | 10. BIRDOSWALD |

Birdoswald Roman Fort, the granaries

can be seen also. The east gate originally had two passages flanked by guardrooms and is one of the best preserved on the Wall. The ditch and earth rampart are best seen outside the south wall. Originally it seems that the bank was fronted by a stone wall with a parapet walk and battlements. The soldiers did not cook in their barrack blocks because of the danger of fire and inside the south gate there are two stone ovens which they would have used. The foundations of the granaries have been well excavated and, as at Ambleside, the walls were supported by massive buttresses. The floors here also were raised to keep the corn dry and again the vents between the buttresses can be seen; these allowed air to circulate and keep the grain dry.

The foundations of some of the other buildings of the fort can be traced and it is believed that there may have been a vicus outside the east wall. A short walk along the Wall to the east leads to the milecastle, Harrow's Scar.

There is an excellent site museum with some of the objects which have been discovered and an interesting interpretation of the whole area.

Directions From Brampton take the A69 going east. Just outside the town, turn left along a minor road to Lanercost, about three miles. At Lanercost turn right. After one mile, the road swings left to Banks, one mile. Turn right here onto the road which runs along the Wall and leads to the fort, about three miles.

11. OLD PENRITH 90 493 385

The fort platform can be seen in the field between the A6 and the river Petteril. The site has not been excavated but many inscriptions and tombstones have been found here, which indicate that there was a vicus outside the fort. Roman roads led from here to the Wall, Old Carlisle and Keswick.

Directions From Penrith take the A6 north. Travel past the Plumpton crossroads, about four miles. The fort is on the

ROMAN FORTS

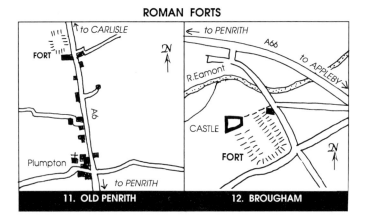

11. OLD PENRITH   12. BROUGHAM

Dacre Castle

Clifton Hall

Cockermouth Castle, the Gatehouse

left, about one mile from Plumpton village.

12. BROUGHAM 90 538 288

The fort platform can be seen with the medieval castle in the north-west corner of the site. A small museum in the castle precincts contains some of the many inscriptions which have been found here. There was a large vicus outside the fort and its cemetery has been discovered nearby. The fort was an important point on the Roman road, High Street, which crosses the fells from Ambleside to Brougham.

Directions From Penrith, take the A66 east for one mile. A minor turn on the right leads to the fort and the Norman castle, on the right after about 200 yards.

13. BROUGH 91 792 141

This fort is situated on a brow above Swindale Beck. The Norman castle was built in the northern half of the Roman site. Part of the fort platform and some of the ditches can

ROMAN FORTS

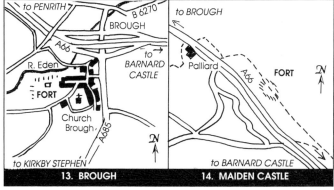

be seen. The fort was situated at an important junction of two routes, one coming across Stainmore from the east and the other going southwards through Ravenstonedale and Mallerstang. It seems that this fort had a particular function as many lead seals have been found in the river below. There may have been some connection with the mines at Alston but this is not yet certain.

Directions From Appleby, take the A66 east to Brough, about seven miles. In the village, turn right to Church Brough. A path from the square near the church leads to the fort and Norman castle.

14. MAIDEN CASTLE 91 792 141
This is a small fortlet in a fine position on an important route. It commands good views of the Eden valley. The shape of the fort can be seen clearly but there is little else of interest.

Directions Take the A66 from Brough east for five miles. 200 yards after a right turn to Keld, the fort is slightly up the hill on the left.

15. LOW BORROW BRIDGE 91 615 758
This fort guarded the Lune gap, the platform can be seen clearly but it is rather difficult to locate. There is little else of interest.

Directions From the village of Tebay, take the A685 south for about two miles. A left turn under the motorway leads immediately to the hamlet of Low Borrowbridge. The Roman fort is on the right, behind some cottages by the railway bridge.

ROMAN FORTS

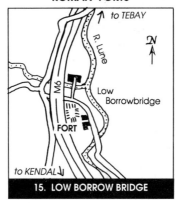

15. LOW BORROW BRIDGE

Three: Norman Mottes and Castles

WHEN WILLIAM the Conqueror had established his rule over the main part of the country, he had to consolidate his position as there could still be opposition to him. One of the methods which he used in this process was to plant his loyal supporters in castles built at strategic points across the country. This was a similar process to that adopted by the Romans so long ago. Indeed, it is interesting to note that many Norman castles are built on the same site as Roman forts and sometimes they are to be found within the Roman camp. At first, the castles were hastily constructed from wood but as the situation became more stable, only some of the original defences were deemed essential and they were rebuilt in stone. Again the similarity to the Roman experience is interesting.

The early wooden castles are called 'motte and baileys' and their remains can be seen all over Europe, although they are especially common in Britain and France. The earliest reference seems to have been in 1010 at Chateau de Langeais on the River Loire where Fulk Nerra, the local lord, constructed one. There may have been a few in England before the Norman Conquest, but most were built after 1066: it seems the Normans were convinced of their strategic importance. About 100 were built by 1100 and many more in the following century.

Like the Roman marching camps, the motte and bailey could be built fairly quickly. After the site was selected, a ditch was dug and a mound of earth was raised within the ditch - this was the motte. A palisade was built round the top of the motte and a wooden tower was erected. At the bottom of the motte, a large flat area was enclosed with a ditch and palisade also - this was the bailey. Every effort was made to make the mottes as strong as possible: some were re-inforced with layers of rock and clay and some had the foundations of the tower built into them. The motte was the last resort - if the outer defences were breached, the defenders withdrew inside the palisade to the tower where they stayed as long as their resources allowed them. Within the bailey were other buildings such as stables, workshops, storerooms and sleeping quarters for the lord's retainers. Because of the ever-present danger of fire, the kitchen was in the bailey, not in the tower. The motte was reached from the bailey by a stepped wooden bridge: this was the only means of entry and could easily be removed in times of danger.

The tower was the most important part of each castle - it was the last defence if the castle was attacked but it also provided the lord with his accommodation. The towers were mostly built of wood. It took at least ten years for the soil of the mottes to settle sufficiently to support a stone building and William's purpose was to establish his authority at once. The tower was a building of some complexity - there were often three storeys stacked above each other. The ground floor provided storage: there was living accommodation on the first floor and probably a chapel and garret rooms for the children and servants on the second floor. Most castles followed much the same plan. Their main purpose was to provide a base from which a small body of mounted men could police a specified area and to which it could withdraw if it was attacked. The simple materials required for these castles meant they could be erected easily and quickly and it is probable that many were not meant to be permanent. The size of both motte and bailey depended on the land available for building and the needs of the particular area: the motte at Brampton in Cumbria is still 130 feet high, some others are much smaller.

Castle-building was undertaken by the king and by his Norman barons. When the king built castles he had a political purpose which was to establish his authority, whereas the barons wanted to guarantee their personal safety in their newly acquired lands. The sites they required were slightly different for the king needed to control the main strategic points in the country. Obvious landing places on the coast could be dangerous and had to be guarded, whilst inland it was important to keep control of crucial fords, passes and defiles on the main lines of communication and military routes. Castles in all such places gave William a remarkable degree of control over his new subjects. The barons built with a similar purpose in their personal estates and no doubt selected sites which gave them maximum security and control over their new tenants.

In any given area, the best site for a castle has to possess certain features. It should give its garrison an unimpeded view of the immediate neighbourhood so that surprise attacks are not likely, it should be reasonably easy for a body of troops to move in and out of it, and it must possess a water supply for times of siege. Some natural features can be helpful for defence and these are utilised where possible. Marsh and water provide good protection and the Normans used these if they were in an appropriate position. Sometimes a stream was dammed to make an artificial lake, sometimes a cliff might be in the best strategic situation - there is a remarkable variety of situations in any region. The disadvantages of wooden towers were soon realised for they could be burnt too easily. When castles were to be retained permanently, their wooden towers were replaced by stone structures and their mottes were razed if they were not strong enough to support a stone tower. The design of the stone towers was similar to that of the wooden towers initially, but eventually many changes were made and some castles became elaborate, complex buildings.

The actual building of a castle was a massive

undertaking. A baron would have been responsible for his own castle, but when a royal castle was ordered, the king's writ was sent to the sheriff of the appropriate county and he had the responsibility of overseeing the tasks involved. Other sheriffs often had to assist with the supply of labour, transport or materials, and the king's need had precedence over all others. The actual building work was supervised by the constable-designate of the castle or an official representative of the king, a very important project was designed by an architect or a military engineer. The main material was a vast quantity of stone as the thickness of the walls of most castles was twelve to fourteen feet or even twenty feet. The expense and difficulty of transporting the amounts needed by horse and cart or even by water were great, so the nearest quarry was always selected. Major quarries were usually owned by the king or perhaps by a monastery so, if necessary, the quarry was hired for a given period or an agreement for a fixed quantity of stone was made. Materials such as iron or lead were also worked as near the site as possible and any materials available from previous buildings were used. It is often possible to detect Roman stone in the walls of Norman buildings.

Building tools were very similar to those used today except that the scaffolding was made of wood. Building usually stopped between Michaelmas and Easter, but occasionally it continued during the winter if the need was urgent, and there are even records of work done by candlelight. Great care was taken to protect unfinished walls from frost for they were intended to last a long time. The cost of the whole operation was carefully recorded and set off against income from the royal estates by the sheriff in his annual audit. Sometimes extra taxes were required or a grant was made from the Treasury.

There are many different castle plans but most incorporate certain main features - they almost all include a ditch, a wall and a tower. Their main purpose was still the same - to provide a base for the most important person in the area so that he could control the people who lived there. At first the stone tower, the keep or 'donjon', was built to a similar design to that of the tower on the motte. The rooms were stacked vertically, three or four main rooms with smaller rooms in the walls which continued above the roof for protection against missiles. The ground floor was the storage basement and often contained a second well. It usually had no direct access to the first floor and was reached by an external staircase or ladder. Obviously this is the most vulnerable part of a building as it can be attacked by undermining or by direct assault, so every effort was made to isolate it in time of siege.

The entrance to the tower was on the first floor and the main hall, the most important part of the castle, was usually here. All public business took place in the hall; the lord received his visitors here, meals were eaten on trestle tables by the whole community of the castle and the ordinary retainers probably slept on benches standing round the walls. Any further floors accommodated the private suite of the lord or his agent. There were tiny private rooms in recesses in the walls but these were not encouraged as they might be a serious weakness. Cupboards and latrines were also built in the walls and the upper floors had fireplaces and some windows. The lower floors had only narrow slits for greater protection; it is possible to see out of a slit and even fire an arrow out of one but it is unlikely to give a substantial advantage to an attacker.

The weakest part of the entrance floor was the door. It was the only point of entry and exit for the whole tower, so every effort was made to maximise its security. The door itself would have been made of stout timber but it could have been strengthened in a variety of ways. Sometimes heavy timbers were added, these slid into recesses in the stone doorway and provided an additional barrier. Iron spikes or bosses could be added for extra strength but the portcullis was the most effective defence. If this iron grid could be lowered in time, it must have given complete protection at this point.

At the time stone towers were replacing the wooden ones, stone walls also took over from the wooden palisade which surrounded the bailey. The 'curtain' walls were at first simple stone walls tall enough to repel the missiles of high trajectory stone-throwing machines. Gradually improvements were made to give assistance to the defenders and the wall became a formidable obstacle. Walls were heightened, a wall-walk was built inside the top and narrow crenels were cut in the parapet to give improved visibility. A good view of the foot of the wall was essential as mining became a successful form of attack. If it was not possible to enter a castle through its doorway, to tunnel under part of its wall was obviously a good means of attack. It became essential for the defenders to be able to see and to attack assailants at the foot of their walls without exposing themselves to arrow-fire. To give a better view, small rectangular towers were built at intervals along the wall. They were often placed at the corners of those structures which were rectangular, as these proved to be the most vulnerable points for this type of attack. After a while, the advantages of round towers were appreciated and rectangular shapes were avoided altogether if possible. The aim was to give the defenders the best field of vision possible and curved towers and walls did just this.

Outside the outer walls, the ditch was also part of the defences. It had to be too wide to leap across and deep enough to be difficult to cross by other means. If it was boggy or steep-sided, so much the better. Only some ditches were filled with water, as a convenient supply was not always available. When siege techniques improved the ditch had to become wider, with high banks and walls.

Some of the stone keeps were massive buildings but there was usually insufficient space for the needs of the lord and all his retainers. Many extra buildings had to be erected in the courtyard within the walls. These were often made of wood and leant against the outside walls. The courtyard provided plenty of space for stables, smithies, workshops of all sorts, and accommodation for the large number of people required to service the castle.

It was not possible for anyone to build a castle just because he had sufficient wealth; permission to fortify a building or 'crenellate' had to be sought from the king. The number of castles in use at any one time varied for several reasons. Any fortification is built when there is some specific danger. Many castles were built after the Norman Conquest in order to control the country and the civil war in Stephen's reign also saw a rush of building as the opposing groups of barons sought to safeguard themselves. On the other hand, Henry II was strong enough to restrict the building of unlicensed castles and even to order the destruction of many which had been built. The potential danger of armed fortresses hostile to the king had always been recognised but only some kings were strong enough to enforce this right.

William the Conqueror demonstrated the way in which it was possible to control the country and the lord in his castle, in charge of the region around it, became a key feature of society for much of the Middle Ages. Castles were used as an important factor in any power struggle until the Civil War in the seventeenth century. However, many changes took place in the methods of fighting, in the weapons used and in the general standard of living in this country and in Europe, which resulted in structural changes in the actual buildings and in the way in which they were used. Eventually cannon-power became too great and castles became redundant but, long before that, other advances in weaponry had resulted in modifications to castle design.

Some alterations were made to the actual structure. Further efforts were made to counteract mining; overhanging galleries were often added to the top of the wall to give a better vantage-point and mural towers became strongholds in their own right. They usually projected from the wall and could control a section of it; often it was possible to enter the ground floor of the tower only from the courtyard and access to the rest of it was from the wall-walk. Strong doors across the wall-walk at different points meant that each tower had to be captured before the castle was finally overcome.

The gateway changed similarly. The simple gap or archway of the early castles gradually developed as different additions were made. As always, the aim was to completely control the flow of all comers. Probably the first improvement would have been to build a passage behind the arch and then the passage itself was often roofed over with timber or stone vaulting. One or more rooms could be built over the passage producing a substantial structure several storeys high. When towers were built either side of the opening, great gatehouses evolved which were often as strong as the keep itself. Although the keep was massively strong, it had certain disadvantages as a weapon of war. While most could sustain a siege for a considerable length of time, they had few means of attack against a determined enemy. The soldiers could not easily emerge from the castle walls and the slits in the lower floors of the towers and the keep were of little use to archers. If the enemy came at close quarters, missiles of varying kinds could be thrown by the defenders, but this was not likely to be very effective. Once again, the rectangular shapes of most keeps favoured the attacker rather than the defender. Some of the same solutions that had been applied to the outer walls were attempted with the keeps. Towers were added to the corners, overhanging galleries were added to the parapet and some keeps were built with a curved or octagonal shape. The shape of the arrow slits was altered to accommodate the crossbow. All these improvements made some difference to the fighting capability of the castle, but it remained essentially a passive tool of war. The attacker could always take the initiative and he had control of the ultimate weapon, the supply of food.

Other problems were caused by the dual use of the keep for civilian life and for war. The original towers had been simply built but, as a higher standard of living was expected, the buildings became much more complex. Special provision had to be made for chimneys and fireplaces, and sanitation and storage were expected. All these had to have recesses in the walls which weakened them considerably. The stacking of rooms inherent in the design led to communication problems, and more staircases were provided but again the strength of the walls was affected. In spite of all the improvements, the keep remained uncomfortable, inconvenient and lacking in privacy. The rooms to which the lord and his family could withdraw became inadequate for the greater demands of the times. Eventually, he was most likely to build a separate, more luxurious dwelling place for his family. This might have been in the courtyard or even outside the walls of the old castle completely. More suitable fortifications were built to accommodate only troops. War became more active, dependent on bands of mercenaries, as it was realised that passive defence did not win battles. Finally the widespread use of powerful artillery demonstrated that even the strongest walls could be destroyed.

Many castles continued to be occupied but increasingly barons relied on the 'King's Peace' rather than their own fortifications for protection. By Tudor times, they built dwellings renowned for their magnificence and comfort rather than for their defensive might. Some castles were used during the Civil War in the seventeenth century but as soon as they were captured by Parliamentary forces, their walls were slighted to prevent further use and many were not occupied again. The King's castles often became prisons and private castles were dismembered, their stone and timber being sold for more modern uses.

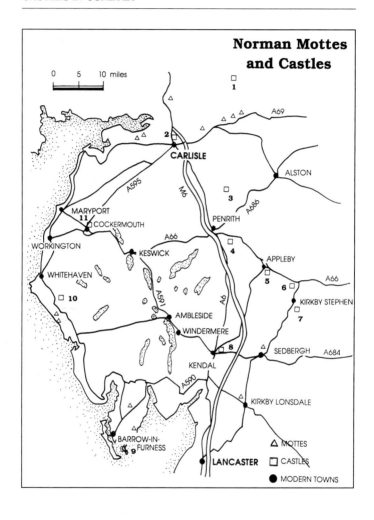

Gazeteer - Norman Mottes and Castles

MOTTES THAT CAN still be seen are marked on the map with a triangle but no map references are given. At first sight some look like part of the landscape but closer examination reveals that they are man made. Some are on private land, so permission from the landowner should be obtained before viewing. Others, such as Castle Howe, Kendal, are now on public land.

1. BEWCASTLE 86 566 747
The castle was founded about 1092 and was built in the corner of the Roman fort on the instructions of William II. It was handed to Bueth, a Saxon or Danish chieftain. It was owned at different times by important Cumbrian families, including the Musgroves and the Dacres, and by King Richard III for a while. It was occupied for a time during the Civil War, when it was reputedly destroyed by a Parliamentary battery from nearby 'Cannon Holes'. It is a shell keep: there was not a separate keep as is found in most castles, but a tower on the west side of the wall and a gatehouse. Not much of the castle survives. An L-shaped ditch isolated the castle from the rest of the Roman fort and this can be traced. The south wall still stands, almost to its original height, and it contains Tudor windows and chimney flues. The gatehouse projects from the west wall and there are fragments of the north and east walls. The most impressive feature is the castle's situation, standing as it does in remote, wild country.

Directions From Brampton take the A69 east to Hexham. At the edge of the town fork left to Lanercost on a minor road, about two miles. At the T-junction past the Priory, turn right. After one mile turn left to Bewcastle, about nine miles.

Open access. Explanatory leaflets can be bought from the adjacent farm.

2. CARLISLE CASTLE 85 396 565

This is the major castle in Cumbria and is in a good state of repair. It played a key role in the defence of the country from Norman times until the accession of James I. The first castle was built by William II in 1092 and the stone keep by either Henry I or David of Scotland. David regarded Carlisle as the southern capital of his kingdom and he actually died there. Whilst the kings of England and Scotland were fighting over the ownership of the north, the castle was attacked by the Scots on several occasions and was overpowered by Alexander II in 1216. It was besieged by Robert the Bruce, but this time the heroic resistance of the governor, Sir Andrew de Harcla, was successful in retaining the castle. Chroniclers described vividly how the siege-machinery of the Scots was stuck in the mud outside the walls.

NORMAN CASTLES

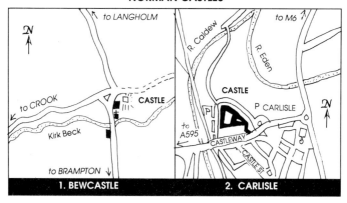

Appleby Castle Photo: Walt Unsworth

Carlisle and its castle were retained by the English henceforth and the castle was occupied by the Warden of the Western Marches. It continued to be a key to the defence of England and was altered and enlarged at different times as needs changed. It remained a prison where unruly Scottish raiders could be held and at least one of them, Kinmont Willie, was removed by his friends in a dramatic rescue. Mary Queen of Scots, started her imprisonment here. During the Civil War, Carlisle was loyal to the king and once again had to endure a siege. Even the Jacobites took the castle for a short time during the 'Forty-five'. However, these later attacks merely confirmed that castles have no reply to the power of artillery. During the nineteenth and twentieth centuries the parade ground and some buildings were used by the local regiment: the castle's role as an important weapon of war was over.

The castle has been altered many times in its long history and only some of its buildings remain. The castle walls and ramparts are in a good state of repair and within the walls are two wards or baileys. The inner ward and keep were built first. When the accommodation they provided became inadequate, the outer ward and other buildings were constructed. The keep is in a remarkably fine state of preservation. It is a grim, massive building which has walls between eight and fourteen feet thick and contains many mural passages and chambers. There are interesting cells on the second floor where prisoners have carved fascinating designs on the walls. A steep ladder leads to the roof and the remarkable view emphasises the good strategic position of the castle. A stepped ramp was built beside the keep in the reign of Henry VIII so that cannon could be dragged up to the ramparts.

Both wards have gatehouses. The outer gatehouse

Arnside Tower Photo: Walt Unsworth

Carlisle Castle

became the residence of the Lord Warden and his household and it has been furnished with reproductions of furniture and fittings, which help to create an image of medieval times. Also in the sixteenth century a half-moon battery was built outside the inner gatehouse on the site of the former drawbridge, and troops with guns could control the outer ward from here. The remains of some other buildings can be seen; in the inner ward are all that survives of Queen Mary's Tower and the foundations of the royal palace and in the outer ward are the small Norman tower where Kinmont Willie was confined and the nineteenth century buildings of the Border Regiment. The King's Own Border Regiment still occupies most of the left-hand side of the ward. Nothing remains of the great hall where Edward I probably held his Parliament in 1307.

Directions The castle is north of the centre of Carlisle and can be reached easily on foot from the central square. Take the road beside the Cathedral, Castle Street, which leads to the Inner Ring Road. After 400 yards the Castle will be seen on the opposite side of the road.

An English Heritage property, it is open all the year but there are special tours of certain parts of the Castle in the summer.

3. KIRKOSWALD CASTLE 86 559 410

This castle was described by travellers as one of the most magnificent that could be seen. Its exact history is not very clear although it is apparent that, like so many great houses, it was owned at different times by various prominent Cumbrian families. Sir Hugh de Morville was given a licence to crenellate his house here by King John. It was destroyed by Edward Bruce after Bannockburn but built again by the de Multon family. Thomas, Lord Dacre, made it into one of his finest strongholds, adding massive curtain walls and a double-towered gatehouse and a great hall with a roof so fine that it was eventually sold to Sir William Lowther. The Howards owned the castle in the seventeenth century when structure seems to have been dismantled and much of its stone, lead and timber sold for

NORMAN CASTLES

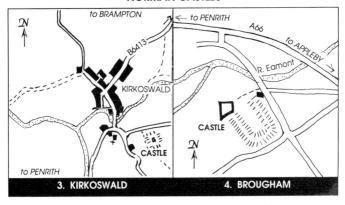

various other buildings in the area.

A small part of the ruins can still be seen. The moat is clearly visible, a fine tower stands on the north side and the remains of twin towers on the south.

Directions Take the A6 from Penrith north to Carlisle. After about five miles, at the Plumpton crossroads, turn right on the B6413 to Lazonby, about three miles. Follow the same road through Lazonby to Kirkoswald, about one and a half miles. Do not turn left on the main road through the village, go straight across the crossroads. The castle is 200 yards along the road in a privately owned field on the right.

4. BROUGHAM 90 537 290

This castle was built within the area of the Roman fort at an important crossing of main roads. It was owned for much of its history by one of the most illustrious Cumbrian families, the Cliffords. The keep was built by Robert de Vipont (c1203-28) but it passed to the Clifford family in 1283. The Cliffords had been border barons in Wales but Robert Clifford made Brougham his principal seat. He was one of the great magnates of Edward I's reign; he was Warden of the Western Marches, Earl Marshall and Lord High Admiral, and was killed at Bannockburn in 1314. He built many additions to the castle so that it became a formidable barrier to the Scots. The keep remained the centre of the castle, but he added a top storey to it to provide apartments and a chapel for his family. He built the inner and outer gatehouses with their unusual escape route to the river.

Robert's grandson, Roger, was also Warden of the Western Marches and he was the next Clifford to oppose the Scots successfully. He made substantial additions to the castle and continued building until his death in 1389. He built a range against the southern and eastern curtain walls which included a great hall, a kitchen and a chapel and joined the hall porch to the keep by a covered way. His castle was hardly altered until the advent of Lady Anne Clifford in the seventeenth century. During the intervening centuries, the castle remained in the Clifford family but had become less important as the danger from the Scots receded. We know it was used as a residence, because there are records of the third Earl of Cumberland being born there and of Kings James I and Charles I staying at different times, but the family seems to have had little interest in it.

The last major building phase was due to the pride of its owner, Lady Anne, in her ancestry, rather than to any lasting, strategic importance. The castle was 'verie ruinous and much out of order' when she took possession of it in 1649 and the aim of the rest of her life was to restore it to its former glory. She must have spent vast sums of money to do this, perhaps to the chagrin of her family, as it was not a fashionable preoccupation at this time. She did not alter the actual structure, but renovated every part and included fireplaces and doorways to make it more comfortable and easy to live in. She spent much time there, when she was not attending to her other possessions, and used the great hall as a courtroom. She was the grand lady of the north-west and was remembered for many years with love and respect. Her heirs, the Earls of Thanet, preferred Appleby, and Brougham was partly destroyed in 1691 and any usable materials were sold in 1714.

The castle was built in red sandstone and remains an impressive sight. The two gatehouses are in a good state of repair and the keep can be climbed to the top. The room on the top floor was octagonal and has the small family chapel leading off it. The Tower of League is diagonally across the courtyard and is in a good state of repair also; the huge well is another feature of this part of the courtyard. The walls of Roger Clifford's range of buildings can be seen, but the most noticeable features here are the remains of the first floor chapel; its elaborate east window, piscina (for washing the sacred vessels) and sedilia (seats for the clergy) are clearly preserved.

Directions From Penrith, take the A66 east to Appleby. After a little over one mile turn right on the B6262. The castle can be seen within a few hundred yards. English Heritage, open all the year, but it is wise to telephone in winter.

5. APPLEBY CASTLE 91 683 199

The first castle at Appleby was built by Ranulph de Meschines in the late eleventh century. This was a motte and bailey built on the banks of the River Eden opposite an existing settlement. He was granted the whole of Cumbria and established a string of castles along the river valley. In 1120, he became Earl of Chester, his northern estates reverted to the crown and they were administered by a sheriff. Then Appleby had a rather chequered history for a time. During the Civil War of Stephen and Matilda,

NORMAN CASTLES

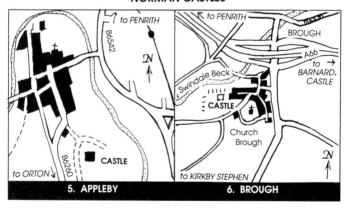

the Scots gained control of the castle but King Malcolm returned it to Henry II. In 1174 William the Lion of Scotland took it again, but Henry II managed to defeat him and fined the constable for surrendering too easily. It remained a crown property until it was granted to the Viteriponts in 1204 and descended to the Clifford family in 1283. It was used as one of the family homes and was enlarged from time to time. It seems to have been neglected in the sixteenth century as there was a report that it was roofless, but in the seventeenth century the remarkable Lady Anne renovated it completely. It stayed in the family until the death of the third Baron Hothfield in 1962 and was sold to Ferguson Industrial Holdings PLC in 1972.

The castle is small, but it is in a remarkably good state of repair. It stands in a strong defensive position above the river and has fine views of the surrounding countryside. The remains of the moat are still water-filled although it is now host to a variety of water birds. Ditches and banks of outer baileys can be seen and the walls are complete. The keep is the oldest building; it is probable that the original motte was destroyed in the twelfth century and was replaced by the present stone keep. The entrance is on the first floor and would have been reached by a ladder which could have been quickly removed. The floors and roof were renewed by Lady Anne, a cross wall was inserted to strengthen the structure and she probably added the turrets to the roof also. There is a separate entrance to the ground floor where the castle well can be seen and narrow spiral stairs to the roof give a vivid impression of the difficulties of life in a castle.

The rest of the castle was developed by the king and by other members of the Clifford family throughout the Middle Ages. In the twelfth and thirteenth centuries a tower and great hall were built against the east end of the bailey, and in the fourteenth century the east range was remodelled as a 'hall house' with square towers at each end of the east front. An impressive arch with a portcullis can be seen outside. In 1422 the sixth Lord Clifford built a great gatehouse on the north side, but only a fragment of this remains beside the present gatehouse. A round tower on the north side shows the Cliffords experimenting with the latest ideas in castle building.

The castle retained its medieval aspects during the life of Lady Anne, but after her death her descendants quickly modernised their ancestral home. The east range was rebuilt by the Earl of Thanet in the seventeenth century style and the Great Hall became part of a comfortable eighteenth century mansion. The Keep and the Great Hall can be visited and in the Hall is the fine triptych of Lady Anne and her family. Lady Anne's bee-house is outside the walls and the grounds contain a collection of rare breeds which is also on view to the public. The remainder of the buildings is used by Ferguson Industrial Holdings.

Directions The castle is at the top of the main street leading from the church of St. Lawrence in the middle of Appleby. It can be visited daily in the summer season.

6. BROUGH CASTLE 91 792 141

Although this castle is a ruin, it is a dramatic sight as it stands on the escarpment above Swindale Beck. It was built within the Roman fort after William II extended his kingdom to Carlisle. It stands at a key point on this important trans-Pennine route. Once again the Normans and the Romans selected the same site for a major defence. Brough remained a royal castle until 1204 when King John granted it to Robert de Vipont. Like Brougham and Appleby, it passed to the Clifford family in 1283 and remained with that family until 1923 when it was quite derelict and Lord Hothfield handed it over to the Ministry of Works.

Because of its important position, the castle was often

Brough Castle

attacked by the Scots. There was great damage after the invasion of William the Lion in 1174 and there had to be much rebuilding. Developments in the thirteenth and fourteenth centuries made the castle sufficiently impressive for Edward I and Edward II to stay here at different times and it was the favourite home of the tenth Lord Clifford, Henry, the 'Shepherd Lord'. It was again derelict when Lady Anne succeeded to her estates and she hastened to restore it to its former condition. Sadly, soon after her death, materials were taken from Brough to repair Appleby Castle and about 1763 Clifford's Tower was partly demolished in order to repair Brough Mill. Thereafter, the battering of the wind and the rain continued the steady process of destruction.

The Norman castle was built in the northern third of the Roman site. It consists mainly of a moat, a keep and a bailey. There is a round tower at one corner (Clifford's Tower) and the remains of some other buildings against the north and south walls. The moat still fills with water

To the Right Hon:^ble

Sackvile Tufton Earl of Thanet,

Baron Tufton Lord Westmorland & Vesey Lord of Shipton in Craven &
Hereditary Sheriff of the County of Westmorland.
This Prospect is humbly Inscrib'd by his Lordships most Obedient Servants
SAM:L & NATH.L BUCK.

when there is heavy rain and the walls are complete. The
keep was built by Henry II to replace the original tower and
was extensively renovated by Lady Anne. There was a store
in the basement with a hall on the first floor and private
apartments on the next two floors. A flat roof was added at
some point as a fighting platform. It is still possible to
climb to the battlements and wonder at the magnificent

BURGH or BROUGH Castle under Staine more, was casually consumed by Fire A.D. 1521, and was rebuilt A.D. 1661 by the Lady Anne Clifford, Countess Dowager of Pembroke, &c. sole Daughter & Heir of George Clifford, third Earl of Cumberland, after having lain one hundred & forty Years desolate. The present Proprietor is y Right Hon.ble the Earl of Thanet.

Sam.l & Nath.l Buck delin: et Sculp: Publish'd according to Act of Parliament March 26. 1739.

view of the Pennines and surrounding countryside. Only the walls of Clifford's Tower remain and only a keen imagination can visualise the courtyard buzzing with activity when the castle was at its peak.

Directions From Appleby, take the A66 east to Brough, about seven miles. In the village, turn right to Church

Brough. A path from the square near the church leads to the castle, which can be seen easily. English Heritage, open all the year.

7. PENDRAGON CASTLE 91 783 026

This is yet another of the castles which belonged to the Clifford family eventually. It was built by Henry II after his triumph over Malcolm III of Scotland, although it is probable that the actual building was done by Sir Hugh De Morville. He was one of the murderers of Thomas à Becket and so was well known at court. The de Morvilles were ancestors of the de Viponts and thus the castle descended to the Cliffords. At first it was a simple tower surrounded by a wall with timber buildings in the bailey; it was extended and strengthened by the Lord Clifford who was killed at Bannockburn and after this was occupied by Lady Idonea de Vipont who was one of the Clifford co-heiresses. It was said to be her favourite residence and she entertained the Scottish king, Edward Balliol, here when he was in exile. She died soon afterwards, and the castle

NORMAN CASTLES

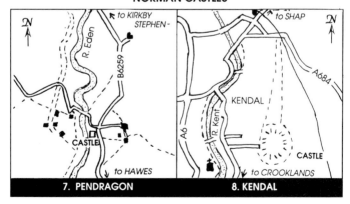

| 7. PENDRAGON | 8. KENDAL |

was frequently attacked by the Scots and declined into ruins until it was rescued by Lady Anne in the seventeenth century. She restored it with her usual skill and delighted in staying here. As with Brougham and Brough, Lady Anne's pride in this ancestral seat was not felt by her heir; he rapidly dismantled Pendragon and it soon became the ruin we see today.

The castle is perched on a hillock beside the River Eden. The Mallerstang Valley was an important route going south and so the castle is in a good strategic position although it does not stand on a hill. Little remains of the actual buildings but originally the keep was three storeys high. The ditches round part of the castle are interesting as they substantiate a local rhyme which connects the castle with Uther Pendragon, the alleged father of King Arthur. He is supposed to have been the lord of a previous castle on the site and the rhyme suggests that he tried to divert the river for the defence of his castle. Pendragon does appeal primarily to a romantic imagination!

Directions From Kirkby Stephen, take the B6259 to Hawes. After about four miles, the castle can be seen on the right. It is in the corner of a field beside the road, at the junction with a narrow lane.

The castle is privately owned but the owner does not seem to object to visitors providing they shut the gate carefully.

8. KENDAL CASTLE 97 522 924

In the twelfth century, a Norman knight, Gilbert Fitz Reinfred, was given permission by Henry II to build a stone castle to protect his lands. He chose the site on the mound east of the river rather than the motte on the hill opposite. Each still stands as an interesting example of Norman defensive constructions. Gilbert married Heloise, daughter of William de Lancaster II and eventually the castle passed through the female line to Sir Thomas de Parr. He was the father of Katherine Parr, the last wife of Henry VIII, and it is thought that she was born in the castle at Kendal. Sir Thomas was a great magnate and was Master of the Wards and Comptroller to the King. It is unlikely that the family visited their northern estates very often, although the income they provided was useful. The Parrs lived at court or on their other estates in the Midlands and south of England. At the death of Sir Thomas, the castle passed to Katherine's brother and he died without issue in 1561. Kendal Castle was not inhabited again and fell into ruin.

It is obvious that Kendal was considered an important strategic position for a long time as we find defences in the area from the Iron Age, from Roman times and from the early and late Middle Ages. Kendal castle is a shell keep; a separate keep was not built as the wall and gate house formed the defence. Much of the wall remains and it encloses an area 250ft in diameter. The gate house is in ruins and great chunks of its masonry have fallen into the moat. The moat is deep and can be followed round part of the site. Five other towers were built on the wall at different times and three of these remain. The square tower was called the Citadel, its walls were five feet thick and partly survive. The vaults of the basement of the Great Hall are all of interest that remain of the south range of buildings.

Directions The castle can be seen easily from the river in the centre of Kendal and a turning from the riverside road leads directly up the hill to it. It is on public land and can be visited at any time but the way up is very steep and can be slippery.

9. PIEL CASTLE 96 234 636

Although the present ruins were said by the historian Camden to have been built in 1327, there was a castle here in the reign of King Stephen in the twelfth century. He granted all his possessions in Furness and Walney to the brethren of the abbey on the understanding that they kept the fort in good repair and defended the area against any enemies who might attack it. There are also records from the time of Henry II indicating that the monks were in control of Piel Harbour and had the task of safeguarding traffic to Ireland. There is little information about the castle after this until the fourteenth century when the abbot, John Cockerham, rebuilt the fort in stone. The abbey was suffering from the depredations of the Scots, as was the rest of Cumbria, and it was necessary to strengthen the defences that were available to the monks and their people. It was particularly important to keep the channel to the harbour open. The monks had property in Ireland and their ships regularly brought in produce from there. In addition, Furness was a wealthy foundation and needed a stronger refuge for its riches when the Scots came on the rampage. The castle was in an ideal position for both purposes.

The castle was intended as a protection for the monks

NORMAN CASTLES

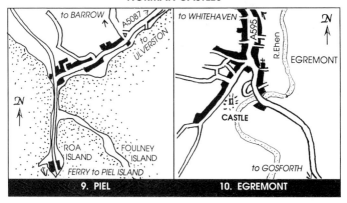

9. PIEL

10. EGREMONT

of the abbey but it gained a reputation as being the refuge of smugglers. Indeed, in 1423, there was an accusation that Abbot Robert himself had been smuggling wool out of Piel Harbour without paying duty. The castle's greatest moment of fame was in 1487 when the Yorkist party attempted to challenge Henry VII soon after he had been made king. They produced the son of an Oxford tradesman, Lambert Simnel, whom, they claimed was the Earl of Warwick. They had him crowned king in Dublin, assembled as large a force of Irishmen and German mercenaries as they could and landed at Piel Castle, intent on defeating King Henry. Lambert held court in the castle and his masters sent out emissaries around the country in the expectation of receiving support. Sadly for all of them, Henry VII was much too strong for the rebels and defeated them soundly in a battle outside Newark. Lambert Simnel disappeared, and it was believed that he drowned whilst trying to escape across the River Trent.

When the monastery was suppressed in 1537, the castle was taken over by the crown and gradually declined. There was some suggestion of repairs when the Spanish Armada was threatening to invade but once that threat was removed interest in the castle declined again. The harbour remained important and the Parliamentarian fleet was anchored there for a while during the Civil War in the seventeenth century. During the eighteenth century the harbour continued as a trading centre but eventually it was eclipsed by Barrow.

The castle was one of the largest in the North West and was built with a keep, inner and outer baileys, walls with ramparts, mural towers and ditches. The outer bailey covers an area of nearly two and a half acres. There are impressive inner and outer gateways, the walls are eight feet thick and the keep measures 80ft by 75ft and is unusual in that the interior was divided into three compartments, each three storeys high. There has been much speculation about the purpose of the middle compartment and also about the way in which these middle rooms were lit. The basement rooms might have been an armoury reached by a ladder but the use of the upper rooms remains a mystery. Part of the walls, the towers and the keep have been washed away by the sea but the ruins remain impressive and the main design of the castle can still be understood.

Directions From the centre of Barrow-in-Furness, take the A5087 to Rampside, about four miles. At the T-junction at Rampside where the main road turns left, turn right through the village. Follow the road across the causeway to Roa Island, about one mile. Here a ferry must be taken to Piel Island. A public house provides refreshments and it is a short walk to the castle.

English Heritage, access any reasonable time but dependent on the ferry which is privately owned. Details can be checked from the Barrow Tourist Information. (Tel: 0229 870156)

10. EGREMONT CASTLE 89 009 102
The present castle was built by William de Meschines about 1130-1140 but there was an earlier Norman motte on a mound to the north of the site. The oldest remains at Egremont belong to the twelfth century. William was a knight at the Scottish court and he built a motte and bailey at the north of the present castle site. He probably added the first stone wall and an outer bailey with a gatehouse. Later in the thirteenth century the castle passed by marriage to the de Lucy family and they made further additions to the structure. They probably built the round Juliet tower, the Great Hall and an inner gatehouse between the two baileys. Further extensions were added along the east wall at a later date.

There does not seem to be anything very interesting

about the castle's history until the sixteenth century, when it was dismantled because its Catholic lord supported the Rising of the North. This was an effort to put Mary Queen of Scots on the English throne and several northern nobles took part in it. Eight years later the castle was reported to be ruined and decayed. It was essentially the seat of the local lord and although it was attacked by the Scots from time to time, it does not seem to have been of great strategic importance to the region and so no great efforts were made to preserve it.

The castle stands on a mound above the River Ehen. The ditches are well preserved and the section north of the gatehouse used to be filled with water from the Brook Well. Part of the wall and the gatehouse are in a reasonable state of repair; only the lower walls of the remaining buildings are visible generally and the oldest stonework has a herring-bone pattern. The massive wall at the end of the outer bailey was part of the Great Hall. The inner bailey is higher than the outer bailey due to the configuration of the site.

Direction From the church on the A595 in the middle of the town of Egremont, take the minor road opposite the church which leads to Middletown. After a few hundred yards, the castle can be seen on open ground on the left. It is between the road and the river.

Access at any time, the castle is on public land.

11. COCKERMOUTH CASTLE 89 124 309

William de Fortibus, a descendant of William de Meschines, was granted the manor of Cockermouth by King John in 1215. There is no clear reference to a castle until 1221, when the Sheriff was ordered to attack and destroy it because of William's insurrection. This was a period when there was great trouble from the Scots: Richard I was more interested in the Holy Land than the north of England but

William the Lion was determined to regain the lands of Cumbria for Scotland. There were many Scottish raids and these resulted in extensive castle building in the region. Kirkoswald and Pendragon were strengthened at this time, Egremont was enlarged, and scholars feel it is quite likely that this is when Cockermouth was first built.

The next building was done by William de Fortibus III in the middle of the thirteenth century. He built on the triangle of land at the confluence of the Rivers Derwent and Cocker. He used the rivers as natural fortifications on two sides of the site and dug a wide ditch on the third side to complete the circuit. There were round towers at each of the three corners and a substantial gatehouse on the east wall. A great hall and a kitchen tower were added in time and there was an outer bailey with a timber palisade. There must have been a drawbridge from the inner gatehouse as it is about six feet higher than the outer bailey.

William's widow died in 1293 without issue and the castle was taken over by the king. In the years that

NORMAN CASTLES

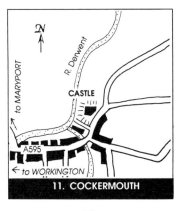

11. COCKERMOUTH

followed it was sometimes administered by a constable on behalf of the king and at other times was granted to a variety of nobles for a limited period, the most famous being Piers de Gaveston, the unpopular favourite of Edward II. At different times orders were made to keep the structure in a good state; money was assigned to repair the walls, the little tower in the inner bailey, the stone wall between the two baileys, the great hall and the kitchen in the outer bailey. The prisons were strengthened and the gates and the engines were overhauled. In 1316 it was reported that 20 men-at-arms, ten crossbowmen and 80 footmen were retained there - Cockermouth was obviously regarded as an important element in the defences of the region.

The castle eventually reverted to the de Lucys, another branch of the original family, and they developed it further in the fourteenth century. The ditch on the east side of the castle was converted into the basement of a range of buildings with a gatehouse in the middle. Dungeons were constructed on either side of the gate with guard rooms above and the kitchen tower in the inner bailey was heightened. The castle was captured by the Scots in 1387 and after this the outer bailey became an important part of the whole structure with stone walls and an imposing outer gatehouse. Henry Percy, Earl of Northumberland, was the lord at this time, due to his marriage to Maud de Lucy, and he placed five shields above the entrance of the gatehouse to illustrate the previous complex ownership of the castle.

The Percys continued to trouble the crown sporadically and at such times Cockermouth Castle was taken over by the crown again. The remoteness of their lands from London perhaps encouraged the Earls of Northumberland to take a very independent attitude to their sovereign - there was even suggestion that Earl Percy was concerned with the Gunpowder Plot. The castle was held for Parliament in the Civil War and was besieged for several weeks by

Cumbrian Royalists until it was relieved by Lieutenant Colonel Ashton, who was sent by Cromwell himself for the task. It seems that the defensive capability of the castle was demolished after this with the exception of the outer gatehouse and it became a stately home like many others. In the eighteenth and nineteenth centuries further ranges were built in the outer bailey and these are the ones occupied today.

The most noticeable part of the castle is the outer gatehouse which is in a fine state of repair. It measures 50ft by 32ft and is three storeys high with a barbican guarding the actual gateway. The barbican was intended as an added protection and had massive walls eight feet thick and 15ft high, although it is not believed that it was ever roofed. There was a drawbridge to the barbican and three gates in the passage leading through the gatehouse - clearly Earl Percy did not intend the Scots to triumph again. The square flag tower is in the south east corner of the outer bailey and the rest of the buildings here are late Georgian and Victorian.

The gate house to the inner bailey also had a barbican. It contains two small rooms which are believed to have been prisons. In each room there is a trapdoor leading to a dungeon known as an 'oubliette', a terrible place in which to be confined. The passage through the inner gatehouse had two gates and leads into the inner bailey. State rooms joined the gatehouse to the kitchen tower. This tower is so imposing that it was once thought to be a keep, but is now known to be the kitchen, having two huge fireplaces and a high roof. It has a basement which was built so elaborately that it had the tradition of being the castle chapel. However, this does seem to be an unlikely situation for religious observations. The Great Hall and the private apartments of the lord lay between the kitchen tower and the west tower. The oldest stonework in the castle is in the basement of the tower and the lower courses of the walls of the inner bailey, but most of the buildings are from a later period.

Directions   From the church in the main street of Cockermouth, walk in an easterly direction. Take a left fork up the hill at the end of the main street, the castle is on the left between the road and the river. It is privately owned but visits are arranged occasionally. Application has to be made to the Egremont Estate Office in the castle.

Four: Pele Towers

PELE TOWERS WERE built mostly during the period after the defeat of Edward II at the battle of Bannockburn. Robert the Bruce and his barons were determined to press home their advantage after this victory and made constant raids into the present northern counties of England. Carlisle suffered the most desperate siege in its history, Penrith, Appleby and Brough were attacked, and Robert even went so far as to cross Morecambe Bay and burn all of Lancaster except for the castle.

The ambitions of kings caused great distress for they frequently devastated the countryside they were trying to acquire, and once the Scots and English discovered there were rich spoils to be gained from each others' territory, families from both sides of the Border followed this example. Numerous expeditions were made into the opposing country, mainly for cattle-rustling although the raiders might take anything else which came their way. Each sortie was planned as carefully as any military operation. These men were unencumbered by baggage or camp-followers, they had an intimate knowledge of the countryside they attacked, and they could travel vast distances burning, slaying and looting wherever they went. It was a way of life for certain well-known families and a very profitable one.

People lived in constant fear of attack. The countryside became so impoverished that the king ordered some of the southern counties to send provisions to the stricken people. Even when a treaty between the two countries was agreed, the raiding continued and some means of protection for people and stock had to be devised. When there was sufficient warning that a gang was approaching, some landowners used to drive their cattle into Yorkshire to safety. For most men it was not feasible to abandon their lands completely, nor was it always possible for whole households to leave their homes, so many English and Scottish knights built small fortifications into which they and their families could retire until the danger had passed.

A simple tower is the easiest structure to defend and these were built in vast numbers on both sides of the present border. In effect they were miniature castles. Some can now be seen standing on their own, while others were developed later and may be detected as part of an elaborate stately home.

The tower was the main structure and had many similarities to the keep of a proper castle. It often stood in a yard or 'barmkin' which was enclosed by a wooden palisade; it had three or four storeys with walls which were as much as ten feet thick and smooth, so that there was no support for the hooks of scaling ladders. They usually had a single room on each floor; the lower storeys were most vulnerable to attack and so they had very small windows whilst the top storey was rather more comfortable as it was the main living-quarter. Newel-stairs were built into the thickness of the walls and usually spiralled from left to right so that they could be defended by a right-handed swordsman. Sometimes a trip-stair might be added as an extra hazard. The top of the tower was obliged to have a cresset fire-basket on its roof as part of the system of beacons for the defence of the region. In emergencies, the barmkin and basement could provide protection for the animals; women, children and the old and infirm were dispatched to the upper floors, whilst the able-bodied men and youths prepared to defend the first floor as well as they could.

There were further similarities to castles. The doors were again the weakest part of the structure and these were defended in a variety of ways. Sometimes iron grilles were fitted in front of the timber and huge bolts and padlocks made a forced entry more difficult for an intruder. The flat roofs of the towers were covered with lead as a protection against fire and as little wood as possible was exposed. Every effort was made to safeguard the inmates and yet give some opportunity for counter-attack. The pele tower was a small fortress but an effective one for raiding parties rarely bothered to besiege them. They entered the tower if they could do so without trouble; otherwise they seized their booty, killed anyone who tried to impede them and departed rapidly. The occupants of the tower often emerged after the danger had passed and carried on with their lives as usual. A small band might follow the raiders in order to retaliate, but generally it was not worth the risk as reivers were ruthless men with little respect for human life.

The towers were only one of the means used to try to safeguard people and property. Sometimes ditches were dug round a building with a bridge as the only means of entry, rather like a moat round a castle. Whole villages or manors might combine to create a communal defence; dykes and ditches were built round a group of buildings with a causeway as the only way in. The earth from the ditches was used to make ramparts edging the causeway and the ground beyond was thickly planted with brushwood, gorse and brambles to make access difficult. Roads crossing the dykes were guarded at night and barred with gates and chains. The enclosure of fields with thorn hedges again made the passage of riders hazardous and even some churches had fortified towers for the refuge of the local populace. Finally there were 'bastles', or 'bastle-houses', the simplest form of fortified dwelling ; these were strongly built stone houses with small windows which are still in use today as farm buildings and are rarely recognised as an erstwhile form of defence.

In spite of the efforts of the Wardens of the Marches, the exhortations of their monarchs and the dangers of their way of life, Borderers continued reiving until the seventeenth century when King James came to rule both countries after the death of Queen Elizabeth I. Even then, many had to be forcibly prevented from continuing their operations. Some of the most notorious families, the Grahams in particular, were removed to Ireland to keep them out of the way. It is said that they crept back quietly as soon as possible, unable to bear the distress of being parted from their beloved country!

When the area became more peaceful, pele towers developed as homes just as major castles did. The first major change was the addition to the tower of a hall or 'aula'. This was a large room where all could meet and where the retainers slept whilst the lord and his family withdrew to their apartments in the tower. The hall was connected to the first floor of the tower by a stairway leading to the dais where the lord dined at the high table. The main part of the hall was at a lower level and the general conditions were very similar to those found in major castles; the floors were covered with rushes, an open hearth provided some heat, the walls were covered partly by wood and perhaps with tapestries if the lord was sufficiently wealthy. A trestle table was set up at meal times so that all could eat together and if there was a minstrel's gallery at the low end of the hall, music might accompany the meals. There was often a door at the end of each of the long walls of the hall and these were joined by the 'screens passage' which served a dual purpose, keeping out draughts and leading to the pantry, buttery and kitchen. There was little furniture in the hall and the retainers slept on benches against the walls. The lord and his lady might have slightly more comfort in the tower, perhaps a bedstead with a straw mattress and some chests to store their possessions.

Some towers had a more elaborate development than this; a second tower might be built at the far end of the hall to give a symmetrical design and accommodate the kitchen and its staff. Sometimes extra wings were added to enclose the courtyard and replace the outer walls and in time the hall itself changed. The lofty one-storey building was divided with a boarded floor built over cellars to bring it level with the first floor of the tower, the hearth was replaced by a fireplace in the wall with a chimney, and windows were enlarged. Once again, as the need for defence receded, more rooms and more furniture gave the tower owners the comfort they expected. The general emphasis changed from the basic provisions of the early, simple towers to the gracious living provided by the typical manorhouse of Tudor times. Sometimes the original tower can be seen from outside as part of the eventual structure, as at Sizergh; in other cases it is hidden by a later façade and only thick walls inside the house give clues to its existence.

The variation in size of the original towers is interesting and so is the extent of the development of some of them; presumably both size and development reflect the wealth and importance of the builders. Obviously, some members of the knightly class were more successful than others. If there was a capable son to succeed his father, an estate was likely to remain in the same family for many generations. We find several of these in Cumbria; the Stricklands at Sizergh and the Penningtons at Muncaster are two examples. Great wealth could be achieved by marriage to an heiress or financial reward could result from service to the king and either could ensure the stability of the family. Indeed, when the distance of Cumbria from London and the difficulty of travelling until relatively recently are considered, it is interesting to discover how many members of this knightly class from the area did hold high office and were rewarded with grants of land by the king. These are the successful families and they tended to have the biggest towers and the grandest houses. The families which did not succeed in this way tended to be poorer to start with, to build smaller towers and to afford only small additions to the tower. Sometimes the names of such families disappear into oblivion for they were part of their county's history for only a short time.

Pele towers are interesting to study as buildings but equally interesting are the family histories which are connected with them. Both made important contributions to the history of the county.

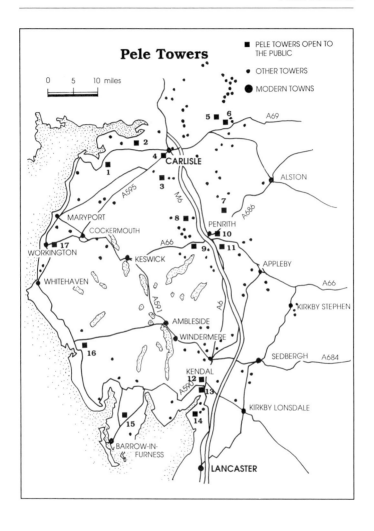

Gazeteer - Pele Towers

THERE IS A wide range of pele towers to be seen in the north west. They varied greatly in their original size and they differ now in the extent to which they have been altered during their history. Some still stand simply on their own like Arnside Tower or Dacre; some, like Dalemain, have been so completely integrated into a later structure that it is difficult to detect exactly which part of the wall was the original tower; yet others can be seen clearly with the later developments attached to them, like Sizergh or Hutton-in-the-Forest. Some are quite derelict and the home of cattle or sheep, while others form an integral part of a gracious home and are still lived in. There is a large number of pele towers - well over one hundred are marked on the map and some may not have been identified yet. Many are privately owned but a reasonable number across the region are owned by public bodies - they can be visited easily and are numbered on the map. Most private owners are very proud of their heritage and some are delighted to share it with others if approached.

1. ST. JOHN THE BAPTIST CHURCH, NEWTON ARLOSH
85 198 553
This is one of the church towers which acted as a defence for the local villagers. As it is close to the Solway Firth, this was an area which was attacked frequently and the church tower is very clearly a fortification. The church was licensed in 1304 and only the tower and nave were built. The only entrance to the tower was from inside the church. The tower had battlements and a turret and the ground floor ceiling is tunnel-vaulted for extra strength. There are small windows in the upper storeys but only a slit at ground floor level.

Directions Take the B5307 from Carlisle to Silloth for about 13 miles to the village of Newton Arlosh. The church is in the main street on the right.

2. ST. MICHAEL'S CHURCH, BURGH-BY-SANDS 85 328 591

This is another church tower built especially to protect the local population. There was a Norman church on the site but the present one was built in the fourteenth century when the Scottish threat was particularly severe. It is similar to the tower at Newton Arlosh with very thick walls and no door to the outside. The basement is tunnel-vaulted also and there are narrow slits instead of windows. The door from the nave to the tower was guarded by a massive iron grille, known as a yatt. The church is built partly with stone from the Roman wall and it stands almost in the middle of the site of the Roman fort Aballava.

Directions Take the B5307 from Carlisle to Silloth. After about one and a half miles, fork right to the village of

PELE TOWERS

| 1. NEWTON ARLOSH | 2. BURGH-BY-THE-SANDS |

Burgh-by-Sands, about four miles. The church is on the left in the main street at the beginning of the village.

3. ROSE CASTLE 85 371 462

Rose Castle is the residence of the Bishops of Carlisle. The manor of Dalston was granted by the king to Bishop Mauclerk of Carlisle in 1230 and it is thought that a house of some sort was built then. The bishops and the priors of Carlisle never had easy relations as the priory was founded before the bishopric and the bishop was almost a visitor in the cathedral, so it was probably tactful for him to have his main home some miles away from the priory!

The original defence was a wooden tower but this was soon burnt by the Scots. Bishop Kirkby was a very warlike incumbent and often joined in expeditions against them which made him much hated. He needed to defend his home and was granted the license to crenellate in 1336, but only portions of the walls he built remain. The oldest stone tower is believed to have been built by Bishop Strickland between 1400 and 1419. Each Bishop seemed

PELE TOWERS

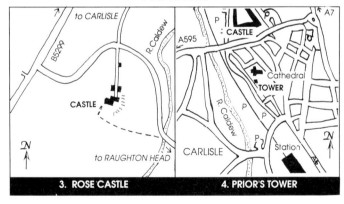

Rose Castle, Strickland's Tower

to feel he had to contribute to the structure and others who followed Bishop Strickland built further towers and a great hall. Eventually the courtyard was surrounded by buildings and the whole site was protected by a wall with a gatehouse.

The Scots continued to attack the castle from time to time but most damage was done to it during the Civil War in the seventeenth century. The castle was occupied by the Royalists in 1648, but they were soon dislodged by the Parliamentary forces who occupied it in their turn. They set fire to the castle when they left and when it was returned to Bishop Stern at the Restoration of Charles II, it was in a poor state of repair. His successor, Bishop Rainbow, had the task of repairing the damage but much stone had been removed from Rose Castle to repair Carlisle Castle during the Civil War and the bishopric could not afford the vast amount of money necessary to restore the whole structure to its medieval glory. Bishop

Rainbow had to be realistic in his renovations and he had the buildings on the eastern and southern sides of the courtyard completely removed. The courtyard was replaced by a lawn and the western and northern ranges were converted into the residence which can be seen today.

Strickland's Tower stands at one end of the northern range and has the usual characteristics of a pele tower. The walls are eight feet thick, the ground floor is vaulted and the original entrance seems to have been at first floor level. There are two rooms and an attic above one another. The rest of the north and west ranges of rooms include the chapel and the drawing room which is renowned for its nineteenth century hand-painted Chinese wallpaper.

Directions Take the B5299 from Carlisle to Dalston. Three miles after Dalston, turn left on a minor road to Raughton Head. In less than one mile, a turn on the right leads to Rose Castle.

Permission to visit the castle by groups at convenient times can be obtained from the Bishop of Carlisle and should be requested in writing.

4. THE PRIOR'S TOWER CARLISLE CATHEDRAL
   85 399 559

This tower is another indication that members of religious orders needed protection from the Scots as much as anyone else. It is part of the cathedral buildings and is just inside the west wall of the city. It provided protection for the Augustinian canons of the priory and has the usual strong walls of a pele tower with massive arches supporting the vaulting of the ground floor. The tower continued to be used as a residence for the prior after the main danger of attack had receded and was altered considerably in the sixteenth and seventeenth centuries. The upper rooms have quite elaborate windows and the first floor solar or day room has a remarkable painted ceiling provided by

Prior Senhouse in the sixteenth century. This was restored in 1976 as it had become encrusted with grime from the main railway line to Scotland which runs below the walls. It is claimed that when the railway was built Dean Close protested strongly that it would encroach on the fine view from his windows. His objections were disregarded, of course, and every time the express passed the tower the drivers sounded their hooters to record their triumph.

Directions The tower is in the cathedral precinct in the centre of Carlisle. It can be visited at reasonable times. Permission to view should be requested from one of the officials on duty in the Cathedral as the tower is kept locked.

5. LANERCOST PRIORY 86 556 637

There are two pele towers at Lanercost Priory but they are not immediately noticed because the priory itself is such a delight. It was founded in 1169 by Robert de Vaux for the Augustinian canons and stands in a beautiful setting by the River Irthing. The Priory was raided by the Scots on several occasions and was said to be impoverished by the fifteenth century. It was dissolved in 1536 by Henry VIII and its buildings were transferred to Sir Thomas Dacre of Naworth. He converted the buildings on the west side of the cloisters into a house and this included one of the pele towers, the Prior's Lodge. The other tower is opposite the west range, at the end of the rectory. It was called King Edward's Tower and is believed to be older than the Prior's Lodge. King Edward I and Queen Eleanor lodged here in 1280 while he was conducting one of his campaigns against the Scots. He stayed here again in 1306 in the last year of his life when he was struggling with illness.

Both towers display the usual characteristics of pele towers; they have the distinctive square shape with smooth, thick walls but have been altered substantially at different times. The Prior's Tower was four storeys high, and is now roofless but it opened on to the hall and was an integral part of Dacre's house. A spiral staircase in the north-west corner leads to the first floor room, where a huge fireplace suggests that this was the kitchen, and another stair in the north-east corner leads to the other storeys. The windows are Elizabethan and little else remains of interest of the original pele. King Edward's Tower is smaller and it also has some later windows. However, the crenellations can still be seen at the top of the walls in spite of the pitched roof and chimney behind them and some of the upper windows are the narrow ones more typical of a pele.

Directions From Brampton take the A69 east. At the edge of the town take a left fork which leads to Lanercost, about three miles. The priory can be seen on the right.

King Edward's Tower is part of the rectory and is occupied by the current rector. The Prior's Tower is part of the ruins of the priory and can be seen at south end of the west range of buildings.

PELE TOWERS

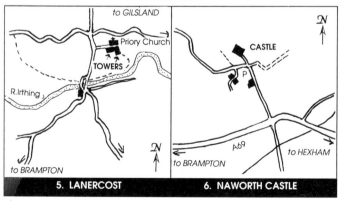

5. LANERCOST   6. NAWORTH CASTLE

English Heritage, access during the summer season at any reasonable time.

6. NAWORTH CASTLE 86 460 359

This is such a splendid building one could be forgiven for thinking it should be included in the section on castles - but it is a pele tower which was developed into a very substantial defensive structure and then into a gracious mansion. There may have been an early wooden tower on the site but the first licence to crenellate was granted to Ranulph de Dacre in 1335 in the reign of Edward III. He built a stone tower (Dacre's Tower) and a stone wall round the courtyard. Thomas, second Lord Dacre, built a further tower (now called the Howard Tower), the Great Hall and the rest of the defences. As the fighting in the Borders diminished, the castle decayed but was transformed when it was taken over by Lord William Howard in 1604. He had married Elizabeth Dacre, one of three heiresses to the Dacre estates, and they made Naworth their home. They converted the castle into a mansion and brought various treasures here from other northern buildings. There were more troubled times when there was a severe fire in 1844 and much renovation had to be undertaken by the architect Salvin. He tried to preserve the medieval character of the castle and much of what we see today is due to his efforts.

The Dacres and the Howards were important families in Cumbria at different times and they were leading figures in local and national affairs. They were often Sheriffs of Cumberland, Governors of Carlisle and Wardens of the Western March. They played vital roles in the fighting against the Scots; William de Dacre accompanied Edward I on his campaigns; Ranulph, Lord Dacre, died at the Battle of Towton where he was supporting the Lancastrian cause, and Thomas, Second Baron Dacre, commanded the reserves at the battle of Flodden. His battle cry 'A Dacre, a Dacre! A red bull, a red bull!' was reported to fill

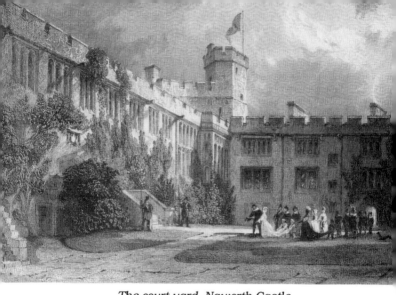

The court yard, Naworth Castle

the hearts of his opponents with dread. Lord William Howard, 'Belted Will', helped to quell the reivers after the accession of James I.

Both familes owned vast estates in various parts of the country which changed from time to time through the centuries due to marriages and deaths. The second Lord Dacre of Gillesland married the heiress Elizabeth Graystock and brought Greystoke Castle into the family. However, the fifth Lord Dacre died unmarried; his inheritance was divided amongst his three sisters and Greystoke Castle became part of the estates of the family of the Dukes of Norfolk. The sister who remained at Naworth, Elizabeth Dacre, married one of the younger Howards, Lord William, and their descendants became Earls of Carlisle. They owned lands in Yorkshire and the third earl had a vast house built there by Vanbrugh. Castle Howard was one of the most splendid houses in the country at the time and Naworth became the family's second home. At the beginning of the twentieth century, family dissension caused the estates to be divided yet again and the two houses were assigned to separate branches; Naworth was inherited by the tenth Earl of Carlisle whilst Castle Howard passed to his uncle, the Hon. George Howard.

The castle stands on land between the River Irthing and the important route from Carlisle to Newcastle. Two small streams were joined by ditches to form a moat and a gatehouse guards the entrance to the courtyard. The two towers are at either end of the south-east front and follow the usual design with smooth, thick walls, vaulted basements and newel stairs. The Dacre Tower has an iron yatt covering the doorway which leads to the dungeons and a guard-turret which rises 17ft above the roof to give a wonderful view of the surrounding countryside. Lord William Howard's Tower has very unusual strengthening in the first floor room and a timber ceiling in the third floor room which was brought from Kirkoswald Castle. The remaining ranges of buildings enclose the courtyard. One side is occupied by the Great Hall which is 78ft long and is the largest in Cumbria. It has a vast fireplace and a dais at one end where the lord sat at High Table, it is hung with French tapestries and contains four remarkable heraldic beasts which hold the family pennants. The Long Gallery contains paintings collected by the ninth Earl of Carlisle. He was a talented amateur artist who was patron to some of the Pre-Raphaelite artists and painted some of the pictures himself.

Directions From Carlisle take the A69 east to Newcastle. After eleven miles and two miles from Brampton, turn left along a minor road which leads straight to the castle. Naworth is the home of the Earl of Carlisle and access is limited. The courtyard, Great Hall, Long Gallery and Old Library can be visited and there is a woodland walk. The castle is open on Wednesday and Sunday afternoons and bank holidays in the summer season and on Saturdays in July and August.

7. ST. CUTHBERT'S CHURCH, GREAT SALKELD
90 552 368

It seems that there has been a church at Great Salkeld for a long time as this is reputed to be one of the sites where St. Cuthbert's coffin rested during its flight from the Vikings in the ninth century. It is not certain when the present nave was built although there is a Norman doorway. The tower was added in the fourteenth century to safeguard the villagers from the raids of the Scots and it is possible that it was ordered by Ralph Nevill, Earl of Westmorland, who was Lord of the Manor of Great Salkeld and built a castle at Penrith at about the same time. Great Salkeld lies on the route through the Eden Valley and it would have been easy to attack. The tower has massive walls, a dungeon with a tunnel-vaulted roof and three storeys above. The only entrance to the tower is through the church and there is a fireplace in the room on the first floor.

Directions From the centre of Penrith, take the A686 to

PELE TOWERS

7. GREAT SALKELD | 8. HUTTON-IN-THE-FOREST

Hutton-in-the-forest

Alston. After about four miles turn left on the B6412. The village of Great Salkeld is reached after about three miles and the church is in the main street on the right.

Access at any reasonable time.

8. HUTTON-IN-THE-FOREST 90 460 359

Hutton-in-the-Forest is perhaps the most gracious of the stately homes of Cumbria. It is the residence of Lord Inglewood and was originally in part of the royal forest of Inglewood. The de Hoton family were hereditary keepers of the royal domain of Plumpton Hay and in return for caring for the deer reserve and the grazing land in the forest and for holding the king's stirrup when he mounted his horse at Carlisle Castle, they were granted the land at Hutton and certain privileges. They were allowed to gather the dead wood and the wood blown down by the wind in the forest, to collect the honey and fruit of the trees known as mast and to capture the sparrowhawks nesting there. These privileges and duties were handed down from father

105

to son over many generations and solemnly recorded, as forest law was important to all the inhabitants of the area and had to be made clear at all times. Edward I visited his forester in 1292 but it was probably Thomas de Hoton, who died in 1362, who built the first tower.

The family name became Hutton in the sixteenth century but its fortunes declined and in 1606 Lancelot Hutton sold the house to Sir Richard Fletcher, a wealthy merchant from Cockermouth. In the eighteenth century, the house passed by marriage to the Vane family and both Fletchers and Vanes played important parts in the life of the county. Several members of the families represented the county in Parliament and Sir Frederick Vane is remembered as the employer of John Peel and the famous hounds. The Vanes remain at Hutton and are still stirrup-holders to the crown.

The pele tower is at the north end of the main block and its thick walls are immediately apparent. The ground floor ceiling is vaulted and there is a spiral staircase in the south east corner and a turret about the parapet. The rest of the house is a remarkable blend of the architectural styles of different periods and is a very good example of how a pele tower can develop into an elaborate mansion. Sir Richard Fletcher began to convert the fortified dwelling as soon as he had purchased it, filling in the moat and building the south front. His son, Henry, continued the extensions with the gallery and cloisters beneath it. Further members of the family continued to extend the house and to improve the gardens and park and in the nineteenth century the architect Salvin was employed to blend the various parts into the charming house we can see today.

There is no record of fighting at Hutton-in-the-Forest and it seems the house became very quickly the admired home of one of the important families of the county. It contains an extensive range of furniture, tapestries, pictures and ornaments and the grounds are similarly impressive. They include a walled garden, terraces with topiary, extensive woodland with walks and an unusual seventeenth century dovecote which contains 4000 nesting boxes.

Directions From Penrith take the A6 going north. After about three miles, at a roundabout, turn left on the B5305 to Unthank and Wigton. The road goes over the motorway and after another three miles the house can be seen on the left. The house is the home of Lord Inglewood and can be visited in the summer season on bank holidays and Wednesday, Thursday and Sunday afternoons.

9. DALEMAIN 90 477 269

There has probably been a settlement on the site at Dalemain since Saxon times but the pele tower was built in the fourteenth century, like so many others. It is very difficult to identify the walls exactly from the outside but inside there is a newel stair in one corner and this would have been the stair of the tower. A hall was added later in

PELE TOWERS

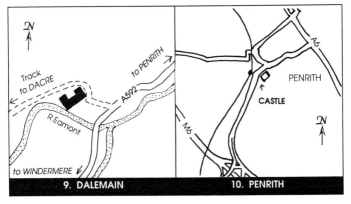

Dalemain - the courtyard

the Middle Ages, there were two wings either side of the hall in Elizabethan times, and in the early Georgian period the house was completed with the present frontage. Ranges of buildings almost surrounded the courtyard and a passage through the great barn leads to a yard with a crenellated wall. This was a substantial fortified hamlet at one time but all the additions to the original tower blended to produce a delightful house with a beautiful garden and interesting farm buildings.

Little is known of the early history of the tower until it was bought in 1680 by Sir Edward Hasell, the steward of Lady Anne Clifford, but no doubt it had provided a safe haven for the local populace in times of danger. The Hasell family has lived here ever since and their house has an attractive collection of furniture, paintings and ornaments. There is an interesting display of agricultural implements in the museum in the barn across the courtyard.

Directions From Penrith take the A66 to Keswick. After about one and a half miles, fork left on the A592 to Windermere. Dalemain is on the right after another one and a half miles.

10. PENRITH CASTLE 90 514 299

Penrith is one of the pele towers which increased in importance over the years but was too close to another fortification, Brougham, to be of lasting importance. About 1380, John de Dreux, Earl of Montford and Richmond, granted to William de Strickland, later Bishop of Carlisle, the perpetual lease of thirty-two acres of waste land in Penrith, Sowerby and Scotby, with the right to build a fortalice (small fort) within the town of Penrith. In 1397 he applied to the king for permission to build a pele tower and two years later asked for a licence to dig stone on the fell to complete the tower and then to surround it with a wall. The licence instructed him to build the tower to protect the town and the adjacent countryside.

The kings at the time must have appreciated the strategic potential of Penrith because when the Bishop died in 1419, Henry V took possession of the fortalice and thereafter constables were appointed to be in charge of it. Several of the constables were leading nobles of the time. John de Clifford held the office for a short while but he had to deliver it to Richard Neville, Earl of Warwick, the 'Kingmaker'. When he was killed at the Battle of Barnet in 1471, the castle and the manor of Penrith were granted to Richard, Duke of Gloucester, later King Richard III. Richard was governor of Carlisle Castle and Lord Warden of the Western Marches at the time, but he lived mainly in Penrith. After his death, lesser men were put in charge and by the middle of the sixteenth century the castle was in ruins. In 1648, Major General Lambert found sufficient cover for his troops for a month but even this was dismantled soon afterwards. The final insult came in the nineteenth century when the Lancaster and Carlisle Railway acquired the site and built the line almost through the middle of the remaining ruins.

The main plan of the castle is square with towers at each corner. It is probable that each of the early constables added buildings to Strickland's original tower within its walls, but it was Richard of Gloucester who made it into a residence fit for royalty. He built another tower, a huge banqueting hall, a porter's lodge, a brewery and a bakehouse. The castle is a total ruin now, its walls remain to an impressive height but only two of the towers can be seen. The foundations of inner walls indicate where the other ranges of buildings would have been.

Directions The castle stands in a public park close to Penrith station on the north-west side of the town.

English Heritage, free access all the year when the park is open.

11. CLIFTON HALL 90 532 271
Clifton Tower is a small tower which stands on its own beside a farmyard. It does not have the massive walls which are usually found in pele towers and it is thought that it was built in the late sixteenth century when the danger from the Scots was less than it had been in previous centuries. The tower was probably built as a home rather than as a defence and so very strong walls were not necessary. The land had been owned by the Engaynes as long ago as the reign of Henry II; they were important people in the region, so it is possible that there was an older, stronger tower on the site before the present one.

The tower and manor passed by marriage to another ancient Cumbrian family, the Wyberghs, and they retained it through the centuries, although they had mixed fortunes. In the seventeenth century there were many problems.

The manor had to be mortgaged to Sir John Lowther during the Civil War; Thomas Wybergh supported the king and had his estates confiscated by Cromwell in 1652: a Thomas Wybergh was taken prisoner by the Jacobites in the 1715 rising; and yet another Thomas was instructed to deliver provisions to Bonnie Prince Charlie when he was on his way south in 1745. The order was issued under 'pain of military execution for non-compliance' and the village and Clifton Hall were plundered for good measure. The tower was used by the family until it no longer provided suitable accommodation.

The tower measures 33ft by 26ft and is three storeys high. It has battlements and a turret at the south-west angle but these may have been included for decoration rather than for defence. The windows are much larger than those of earlier pele towers and the ground floor was divided into a number of rooms, both signs of calmer times. There is a newel stair in the south-west angle leading to the upper rooms and the roof and traces of other buildings adjoining the tower can be seen but these were

PELE TOWERS

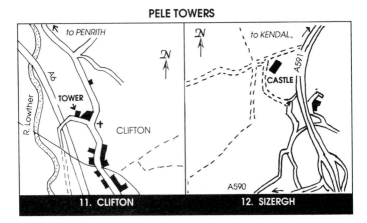

11. CLIFTON   12. SIZERGH

destroyed long ago.

Directions Take the A6 south from Penrith for two miles to the village of Clifton. The tower is on the right along a farm lane at the beginning of the village.

English Heritage, access all the year.

12. SIZERGH CASTLE 97 545 837

The development of a pele tower into a splendid mansion can be seen very clearly at Sizergh Castle. The pele tower is a very large one, sixty feet by forty feet, and it stands four storeys high in one corner of the present building. It is easy to see how the hall was built on to the tower and then two wings were added at right-angles to provide extra accommodation.

Sizergh belonged to the Strickland family until it passed to the National Trust in 1950. The lands were granted by Henry II to Gervase Deincourt of Lincolnshire about 1170 and remained in that family until 1239 when the sole heir, Elizabeth, married Sir William Strickland. The Stricklands were distinguished in many spheres of public service throughout their history and were granted the right to enclose their lands and maintain a deer park, which they did until the eighteenth century. They were knights of the shire and members of thirty-one Parliaments between 1290 and 1928, they fought in many battles with distinction in Scotland, France and Ireland and were faithful servants of the crown. Several of the family were rewarded for their service: in 1306 Sir Walter was made a Knight of the Bath, and in 1415 Sir Thomas carried the banner of St. George at the Battle of Agincourt.

The Stricklands always remained Catholic and devotion to the Royal Family and the Catholic Church resulted in a drastic reduction in the family fortunes in the seventeenth century. Sir Thomas and his wife Winifred were members of the household of James II and Mary of Modena and when they abdicated in 1688, the Stricklands followed the king and queen into exile. Much of the family fortune was lost at this time and when their son Walter was allowed to return to England at the end of the century, he lived quietly in reduced circumstances for the rest of his life. Further marriages in the family brought more land and wealth at times and members of the family continued to serve their country with distinction, as their ancestors had done.

The pele tower at Sizergh is one of the largest in Cumbria and was built about 1350. It is 58ft high and has battlements at roof level and two projecting turrets which are ten feet higher. The turret on the south side is called the Deincourt Tower and it contained the garderobes; the other turret is hidden by the hall block and it contained the stairs. The walls of the tower are massive; they are more than nine feet thick at ground level and smooth on the outside, as is usual in pele towers. Large windows have been inserted in the tower at various times, but some of the original slits remain. The basement is tunnel-vaulted and a low doorway, which is now on the ground floor, was the only entrance. The doorway leads also to the newel stair, which was the only way up to the other floors and the roof. Each floor contained one large room, but most of the rooms were divided in later centuries to provide extra accommodation. The floor at the top was used as a lumber room for many years and it must be largely unaltered from its original condition.

The Great Hall was added about 1450 and at that time would have extended up to an open, timbered roof. In Elizabethan times Sir Walter Strickland rebuilt the Hall. It was given a wooden floor raised over cellars almost to the level of the first floor of the pele tower and was enlarged to provide a forty-foot square room of some splendour. Sir Walter also added external stairs as the main entrance to the house and a block at the far end of the hall. This had tunnel-vaulted cellars and a newel-stair similar to those of the original pele tower. Many of the rooms were panelled and fine fireplaces with elaborate overmantels were installed. Wings were added to both ends of the main structure in the sixteenth century, partly by the same Sir Walter, and these provided workshops, kitchens and yet more bedrooms. On the first floor of the south wing was a room 118ft long where, it is said, he kept a fully equipped company of 290 men.

Further changes were made to parts of the structure in the eighteenth and nineteenth centuries as fashions in buildings changed. In the eighteenth century, Charles Strickland married an heiress, Cecilia Townely, and she used her great wealth to make some drastic alterations. She had the Great Hall and its outer stairs replaced by a three storey block and introduced large Venetian-style windows. The porch and the windows either side of it were added in the nineteenth century.

The house contains a fine collection of furniture, pictures and ornaments which belonged to the Strickland family and much of the Elizabethan panelling and the fine fireplaces remain. Evidence of a moat can be detected on three sides of the building and there is a charming garden.

Directions From Kendal take the A6/A591 south. After about three miles, at a major intersection turn right ont) the A590 to Barrow-in-Furness. After a few hundred yards, a small lane on the right leads to the castle.

National Trust, open Monday, Wednesday, Thursday and Sunday afternoons in the summer season.

13. LEVENS HALL 97 499 851

Levens Hall was owned for many centuries by another of the prominent families of Westmorland, the de Redmans. The first member of the family, Norman de Hieland, was granted land at Levens in about 1170 and his descendants lived here until the house was sold in 1562. The de

Redmans were soon important people in the area as documents at the end of the twelfth century show that Sir Henry de Redman was seneschal of Kendal and sheriff of Yorkshire. Seven of the de Redmans who succeeded Henry through the centuries were called Matthew, so it is not always easy to distinguish one from another, but all continued to serve the country in local government and in war. It was probably the second Sir Matthew who attended a military council in London with Prince Edward in 1297 and in 1299 he supported Lord Clifford in the Borders against the Scots. He was member of Parliament for Westmorland and when he was Commissioner for Array in Lancashire and Westmorland, he raised a force of two hundred footmen. He was even sheriff of the castle at Dumfries at one time and continued to be present at all major battles until 1324 when he attended the great council in Westminster. He was obviously a man of considerable importance.

It was probably Sir Matthew III who built the first pele tower and hall and Sir Matthew IV who enclosed the park

PELE TOWERS

to KENDAL
to BARROW
R. Kent
HALL
A6
to LANCASTER
13. LEVENS HALL

to ARNSIDE
N
Farm
TOWER
FAR ARNSIDE
Morecambe Bay
to SILVERDALE
14. ARNSIDE TOWER

in 1360. Sir Matthew III was in charge of the ports in Cumberland and Westmorland and had to ensure that no supplies from them reached the Scots. He was also sheriff of Cumberland and governor of Carlisle Castle as well as representing Westmorland in Parliament. Sir Matthew IV fought in France with John of Gaunt and was Warden of the Western Marches for a while. Sir Richard I was very prominent in public affairs and as well as performing the usual local functions to which the de Redmans were accustomed, he was commissioned to negotiate with the Scots on several occasions and in 1415 he was appointed Speaker of the Parliament which sat at Northampton. Sir Richard married an heiress from Yorkshire, Elizabeth Stapleton, and from this time the de Redmans became equally interested in their Yorkshire property, Harewood Castle.

The family fortune declined in the sixteenth century and Levens Hall was sold in 1562 to Sir James Bellingham. His son James remodelled the old pele tower and the present house is the result of his efforts. He added a dining room, drawing room, servants quarters and built-in kitchens, and embellished the house with panelling, plaster work and tapestries in the manner of the time. In the seventeenth century, the house was sold to Colonel James Graham who also lavished much time and money on improvements. He built the south wing and bought some fine furniture but his most notable achievement was the creation of the gardens. For this purpose he brought to Levens the royal gardener, Monsieur Beaumont, who had trained at Versailles. The house passed in time by marriage to the Howard family and finally to the Bagots who live in it now.

Levens Hall is another fine example of a pele tower which has developed into a gracious mansion and it incorporates building styles of several different periods. The original tower is on the left of the present entrance and has the usual vaulted basement. Another tower on the right of the entrance was added when the banqueting hall was raised over cellars. The rooms which are open to the public contain an impressive collection of furniture, pictures and ornaments. The topiary in the garden is amongst the finest in the country and across the road is an attractive deer park.

Directions From Kendal take the A6 south. After about three miles, turn at the major intersection on to the A6, A59T (Milnthorpe and Barrow). After about one mile, take a slip road left A6 to Milnthorpe, Levens Hall is on the corner at the next junction 2 miles north of Milnthorpe.

The house is occupied by the Bagot family but is open to the public during the summer season on Tuesdays, Wednesdays, Thursdays, Sundays and bank holidays. There is a public access to the deer park by a footpath at all times.

14. ARNSIDE TOWER 97 488 768

Arnside Tower is in a magnificent position guarding a valley which leads inland from Morecambe Bay below Arnside Knott. It stands on high ground above the adjacent farm and is now a ruin but still presents a remarkable sight. In its heyday, it must have dominated the locality. There is little certainty about its history but it is believed that it was built by the de Broughton family in the fourteenth century. There is a legend, which may have some truth, that it was constructed, along with towers at Hazleslack and Dallam, for the three sisters of Thomas de Thivery. There is a reference in the Lancaster Parish Register of 1602 that the Tower was burnt down and rebuilt. It was owned by the Earls of Derby for a considerable time and seems to have been occupied until 1690, when lead and timber were removed and sent to Knowsley. It was sold in 1815 to Daniel Wilson of Dallam Towers.

The tower stands on its own, is built of limestone and is fifty feet high and almost as long. The walls are four to five feet thick and the main block was four storeys high with a turret which was used for garderobes. The tower was strengthened by a cross wall and a spiral stairway leads to the battlements. There is a vaulted oven in the basement of the turret which shows where the kitchen was. The hall was on the second floor.

Directions From Kendal take the A6 south to Milnthorpe, about six miles, at the traffic lights turn right on the B5282, about three miles. At the T-junction with the coastal road turn left. After half a mile take the first turn on the right, then the second turn on the left to Silverdale. Arnside Tower will be seen on the left after a little over half a mile. It is possible to go down the lane to the adjacent farm in order to reach the tower.

15. DALTON CASTLE 96 230 740

Dalton-in-Furness was the chief town and administrative centre for the Furness region for a long time. When Furness Abbey was founded in 1127, the monks needed a building in which to hold their manor courts and to use as a prison for criminals captured within the jurisdiction of their Liberty of Furness. There must have been some such building quite soon afterwards as a court house and a prison are referred to in a document of 1257. The present tower contained both but was not built until the fourteenth century, no doubt as a result of the attacks of Robert the Bruce in the area. The tower was used as a prison until 1774 and the manor court was held in the tower until 1925 when the Law of Property Act abolished such courts.

The monks of Furness Abbey were responsible for the upkeep of the building until the dissolution of the monasteries in the sixteenth century when they had to forfeit all their property to the crown. It seems that Dalton

Castle fell rapidly into disrepair for, in 1546, it was reported to be 'in great ruin'. The king's bailiff, William Sandes, was ordered to repair it and he used materials from the deserted abbey for this purpose. Extensive alterations were made to the building in the eighteenth century when part of the ground floor was made into stables and further minor changes were made throughout the century. The next major reconstruction took place in 1856 when the interior was entirely remodelled and the three original storeys were replaced by two. A new roof was installed in 1907 to create the building we can see today. In these later years the tower had been part of the estates of the Duke of Buccleugh, but in 1968 it was taken over by the National Trust. The court was held in the upper floor of the present building and was on the first floor of the old building.

The tower measures 45ft by 30ft and is 40ft high to the top of the parapet. It is built of limestone with red sandstone dressings and the walls are six feet thick and nine feet where there is a mural passage at the foot of the

PELE TOWERS

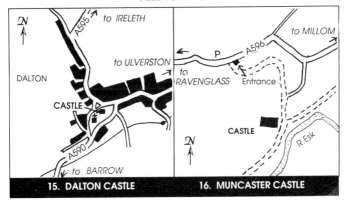

15. DALTON CASTLE | **16. MUNCASTER CASTLE**

stairs. The parapet is five feet high, projecting six inches from the walls, which is unusual in a pele tower, and has several loops for the discharge of missiles. The original three storeys were connected by a newel stair in the west wall and the stair also is unusual, as it winds from right to left rather than from left to right. No reason is known for this, although similar stairs were built elsewhere to accommodate left-handed swordsmen. There are slits in the external walls to light the stairs and the mural passage and there is a dungeon under the north room on the ground floor. The corbels which supported the original floors can be seen, otherwise the interior remains as it was reconstructed in 1856.

Directions From Barrow-in-Furness, take the A590 to Ulverston. Dalton-in-Furness is reached after four miles, Dalton Castle is in the old market place on the main road.

National Trust, the castle can be visited by applying to the local custodian. The directions are on the castle door.

16. MUNCASTER CASTLE 96 104 964

Muncaster Castle is one of the most attractive stately homes of Cumbria. It stands on a wooded spur overlooking the River Esk near Ravenglass and is in a fine strategic position. Nowadays it is famed for its delightful rhododendron gardens and its wonderful views over the Lake District. The house is still owned by the descendants of the Penningtons, the family which built the first tower here. Some of the Penningtons were referred to as 'de Mulcastre' and in the eighteenth century Sir John Pennington was elevated to the peerage and there are several lords in the family tree. The lands above Ravenglass were granted to Alan de Penitone in 1208; Gamel de Mulcastre built a castle here fifty years later and the pele tower was constructed in the fourteenth century. The tower was probably extended gradually, as was the custom, but little remains of the early structure. It was rebuilt in 1783 by John, first Lord Muncaster, and then remodelled entirely by the architect Salvin for the fourth Lord Muncaster in 1862-3. The house we see today is almost totally the work of Salvin, but parts of the ancient pele tower can be seen inside.

The Penningtons played a prominent part in the life of West Cumberland, as would be expected. In the thirteenth century, Robert de Mulcastre was High Sheriff of Cumberland and in 1291 Walter de Mulcastre was the first recorded Member of Parliament for the county. However, the family's greatest claim to fame occurred during the Wars of the Roses when Sir John Pennington and his wife entertained King Henry VI in their home. As a token of his gratitude the King gave then a gift, a cup now called the 'Luck of Muncaster', with the prophecy that the family would prosper as long as the cup remained unbroken in its possession. It is still the family's greatest treasure. Three years later the family again gave shelter to the King, but this time he was a fugitive after being defeated at the Battle of Hexham. Henry was found wandering on the fells by a shepherd who brought him to the house where he was entertained by the family, as he had been in happier days. In 1783 John, Lord Muncaster, erected a tower, now called Chapels, on the spot about a mile away where shepherd and king encountered one another.

The pele tower cannot be distinguished externally from Salvin's façade but internally the usual characteristics of a pele tower are apparent. The walls are eight feet thick and the ground floor is tunnel-vaulted. There are two spiral stairways; one leads to the first floor only, whilst the other continues to three further floors. The rest of the house is Salvin's interpretation of an historic mansion and contains an interesting collection of furniture, paintings and ornaments. In addition to the castle gardens, is a fine terrace which extends along the hillside for half a mile.

Directions From Whitehaven, take the A595 south to Ravenglass. Do not take the right turn into the village but follow the main road up the hill for a further half a mile. The drive to Muncaster Castle is on the right, a car park is on the opposite side of the road.

The castle is privately owned and is the home of Mrs Gordon-Duff-Pennington. It is open to the public in the summer season every day except Monday and on bank holidays.

17. WORKINGTON HALL 89 008 288

Workington Hall was the chief residence of yet another famous Cumbrian family, the Curwens. They could trace their descent from King Malcolm II of Scotland and King Ethelred of England. Patric de Culwen settled on this site, and his great-grandson built the first stone tower here. Licence to crenellate was granted in 1380 by King Richard II. Sir Christopher Curwen was Lord of Westmorland for nearly fifty years and he fought at the Battle of Agincourt with Henry V. It was probably he who added the first hall

PELE TOWERS

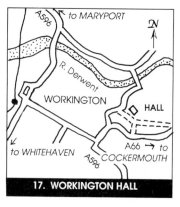

17. WORKINGTON HALL

Workington Hall

to the original tower and perhaps he added the gatehouse also. In Tudor times Sir Thomas Curwen was an important man; he was on good terms with King Henry VIII and was given Shap Abbey and its lands when the monasteries were dissolved. By chance it had been founded by one of his ancestors.

The hall's greatest moment of fame came in the sixteenth century when Sir Henry Curwen and his wife had to entertain Mary Queen of Scots. She had just fled from Scotland and Workington Hall was the first of the many residences she occupied during her long struggle to survive. Naturally she was treated by Sir Henry with the deference due to her rank but perhaps he was not surprised to receive a letter from Queen Elizabeth I with detailed instructions. Elizabeth recognised the importance of Mary's rank and emphasised that she must be treated correctly, but she was adamant also that Mary and her entourage must on no account be allowed to escape. The exiled queen showed her gratitude to the Curwens for their care of her and gave them an agate cup. Her bedroom was known ever after as 'The Queen's Room'.

The Curwens continued to be prominent members of the community and to take an active part in local affairs. The hall was extended further at the end of the sixteenth century when two more wings were built to enclose the courtyard and it became a stately Elizabethan mansion. In 1782 and 1828 still more additions resulted in the building we can see today; these included a library, flanking corridors round the courtyard and renovations to the tower. In 1946 the hall was presented to the town of Workington by the Lady of the Manor, Mrs Chance. For a considerable time it was allowed to sink into a state of decay, but now Allerdale Council has started on a programme of conservation, so what remains of this remarkable house should be preserved for posterity.

Only the outer walls remain but most of them stand to almost their original height and are an impressive sight. The pattern of the house can be understood easily as the ranges of buildings still enclose the courtyard. The pele tower is in the south east corner and has a vaulted basement and the gatehouse is also reputed to be medieval and is very well preserved. There was a large Tudor hall which was reached by a double staircase from the courtyard.

Directions From the centre of Workington take the A66 to Cockermouth. On the edge of the town on the left of the main road is a large park in which the hall stands.

The hall is owned by Allerdale Council, the park is open at all normal times and the house is open every day during the summer season.

The south view of Lowther Castle, a grandiose Gothic house replacing an earlier castle. Formerly the seat of the Earls of Lonsdale it is now an empty shell, not open to the public. The long north front can be seen from the minor road which joins Askham to the A6

CICERONE GUIDES

Cicerone publish a wide range of reliable guides to walking and climbing in Europe

FRANCE
TOUR OF MONT BLANC
CHAMONIX MONT BLANC - A Walking Guide
TOUR OF THE OISANS: GR54
WALKING THE FRENCH ALPS: GR5
THE CORSICAN HIGH LEVEL ROUTE: GR20
THE WAY OF ST JAMES: GR65
THE PYRENEAN TRAIL: GR10
TOUR OF THE QUEYRAS
ROCK CLIMBS IN THE VERDON

FRANCE / SPAIN
WALKS AND CLIMBS IN THE PYRENEES
ROCK CLIMBS IN THE PYRENEES

SPAIN
WALKS & CLIMBS IN THE PICOS DE EUROPA
WALKING IN MALLORCA
BIRDWATCHING IN MALLORCA
COSTA BLANCA CLIMBS

FRANCE / SWITZERLAND
THE JURA - Walking the High Route and Winter Ski Traverses
CHAMONIX TO ZERMATT The Walker's Haute Route

SWITZERLAND
WALKS IN THE ENGADINE
THE VALAIS - A Walking Guide
THE ALPINE PASS ROUTE

GERMANY / AUSTRIA
THE KALKALPEN TRAVERSE
KLETTERSTEIG - Scrambles
WALKING IN THE BLACK FOREST
MOUNTAIN WALKING IN AUSTRIA
WALKING IN THE SALZKAMMERGUT
KING LUDWIG WAY

ITALY
ALTA VIA - High Level Walkis in the Dolomites
VIA FERRATA - Scrambles in the Dolomites
ITALIAN ROCK - Selected Rock Climbs in Northern Italy
CLASSIC CLIMBS IN THE DOLOMITES
WALKING IN THE DOLOMITES

OTHER AREAS
THE MOUNTAINS OF GREECE - A Walker's Guide
CRETE: Off the beaten track
Treks & Climbs in the mountains of RHUM & PETRA, JORDAN
THE ATLAS MOUNTAINS

GENERAL OUTDOOR BOOKS
LANDSCAPE PHOTOGRAPHY
FIRST AID FOR HILLWALKERS
MOUNTAIN WEATHER
MOUNTAINEERING LITERATURE
THE ADVENTURE ALTERNATIVE

CANOEING
SNOWDONIA WILD WATER, SEA & SURF
WILDWATER CANOEING
CANOEIST'S GUIDE TO THE NORTH EAST

CARTOON BOOKS
ON FOOT & FINGER
ON MORE FEET & FINGERS
LAUGHS ALONG THE PENNINE WAY

(ɕ) CICERONE PRESS

Also a full range of guidebooks to walking, scrambling, ice-climbing, rock climbing, and other adventurous pursuits in Britain and abroad

Other guides are constantly being added to the Cicerone List.
Available from bookshops, outdoor equipment shops or direct (send for price list)
from CICERONE, 2 POLICE SQUARE, MILNTHORPE, CUMBRIA, LA7 7PY

CICERONE PRESS BOOKS

Cicerone publish a range of guides to walking and climbing in Britain and other general interest books

LAKE DISTRICT
LAKELAND VILLAGES
WORDSWORTH'S DUDDON REVISITED
REFLECTIONS ON THE LAKES
THE WESTMORLAND HERITAGE WALK
THE HIGH FELLS OF LAKELAND
IN SEARCH OF WESTMORLAND
CONISTON COPPER MINES - A Field Guide
CONISTER COPPER - A History
SCRAMBLES IN THE LAKE DISTRICT
MORE SCRAMBLES IN THE LAKE DISTRICT
WINTER CLIMBS IN THE LAKE DISTRICT
THE REGATTA MEN
LAKELAND - A Taste to Remember. (Recipes)
THE CHRONICLES OF MILNTHORPE
WALKS IN SILVERDALE/ARNSIDE - Area of
Outstanding Natural Beauty
BIRDS OF MORECAMBE BAY
THE EDEN WAY
OUR CUMBRIA
PETTIE (Memories of a Victorian Nursery)

NORTHERN ENGLAND
THE YORKSHIRE DALES
WALKS IN THE YORKSHIRE DALES
LAUGHS ALONG THE PENNINE WAY
 (Cartoons)
THE RIBBLE WAY
NORTH YORK MOORS
WALKING THE CLEVELAND WAY AND
MISSING LINK
WALKS ON THE WEST PENNINE MOORS
WALKING NORTHERN RAILWAYS
Vol.1. East Vol.2. West
BIRDS OF MERSEYSIDE
ROCK CLIMBS IN LANCASHIRE AND THE
 NORTH WEST
THE ISLE OF MAN COASTAL PATH
HERITAGE TRAILS IN N.W. ENGLAND
THE LANCASTER CANAL

DERBYSHIRE PEAK DISTRICT
WHITE PEAK WALKS Vol. 1 & 2
HIGH PEAK WALKS
WHITE PEAK WAY
KINDER LOG

WALES
THE RIDGES OF SNOWDONIA
HILL WALKING IN SNOWDONIA
ASCENT OF SNOWDON
WELSH WINTER CLIMBS
MOUNTAIN SUMMITS OF WALES
SNOWDONIA , WHITE WATER, SEA & SURF

WELSH BORDER
ROCK CLIMBS IN THE WEST MIDLANDS

SOUTH & WEST ENGLAND
WALKS IN KENT
THE WEALDWAY & VANGUARD WAY
THE SOUTH DOWNS WAY & DOWNS LINK
WALKING ON DARTMOOR
SOUTH WEST WAY - Vol. 1 & 2
THE COTSWOLD WAY

SCOTLAND
SCRAMBLES IN LOCHABER
SCRAMBLES IN SKYE
ROCK CLIMBS: GLEN NEVIS & LOCHABER
 OUTCROPS
THE ISLAND OF RHUM
CAIRNGORMS, WINTER CLIMBS
WINTER CLIMBS BEN NEVIS & GLENCOE
SCOTTISH RAILWAY WALKS
TORRIDON

**CICERONE
PRESS**

Also a full range of guide-books to walking, scrambling, ice-climbing, rock climbing, and other adventurous pursuits in Britain and abroad.

Available from bookshops, outdoor equipment shops or direct (send for price list) from: CICERONE PRESS, 2 POLICE SQUARE, MILNTHORPE, CUMBRIA LA7 7PY

Printed in Gt. Britain by
CARNMOR PRINT & DESIGN
95-97 LONDON RD. PRESTON